# AI REVOLUTION FOR LINKEDIN PROFESSIONALS

AN ACTIONABLE PLAYBOOK TO AUTOMATE OUTREACH, GENERATE LEADS, AND MASTER THE EXACT AI TOOLS YOUR COMPETITION IS USING TO WIN

AI REVOLUTION

BOOK 1

HEIDI WINKLER

WINKLER PUBLISHING

# CONTENTS

# FOREWORD

I'm not going to lie...I came to AI kicking and screaming, and it was Heidi Winkler, the author of this brilliant tome, who helped me demystify one of the most transformative technologies of our time.

As I worked with Heidi to create AI training videos for our Sales team, she took me from drowning in the fear of using AI to making me a believer. As I worked with Heidi, she showed me how easy it is to reshape how we communicate and how to do so more effectively. And then she wrote this book, which I've just finished reading.

Here, Heidi clearly walks the reader through the "What," "Why," and most importantly, the "how" of using AI in our everyday lives to make our businesses more successful. Heidi includes actionable advice as she shows us why it is no longer an option to avoid AI — it's here and it's staying.

***The LinkedIn Professional's AI Toolkit*** is a powerful tool that helps us stay ahead of the curve, inspires confidence in ourselves, and sparks important ideas as it empowers us. With this book, Heidi removes any fear of AI as a threat, and this review is coming from a person who was scared to death of AI. I am so happy that Heidi helped me learn to understand and use this important tool.

Sherri Cortland, ND

Project Manager

Global Connections, Inc.

# THE AI REVOLUTION IN PROFESSIONAL LIFE

WELCOME TO THE AI ERA—WHERE YOUR COFFEE MAKER might just be more innovative than your high school guidance counselor, and your inbox is probably filling with AI-generated emails that make you wonder if your colleagues actually wrote them. Even my dog, Bernie, a charming Bernedoodle who has somehow become a minor LinkedIn celebrity, has grasped the concept faster than some seasoned professionals (though he's still working on his typing skills).

If you've spent any time on LinkedIn lately, you've seen the AI gold rush in action. Marketers are cranking out entire campaigns in minutes, sales reps are automating their prospecting, and content creators? Well, they're either thrilled or nervously refreshing job listings. Lawyers, doctors, and educators are cautiously testing the waters with AI, unsure if it's a trusted companion or a liability waiting to wreak havoc—much like Bernie during a thunderstorm.

But let's get real—AI isn't on its way; it's already here. Sitting beside you, quietly revolutionizing your workflow, and occasionally making embarrassing mistakes you'd prefer not to admit to your boss. The professionals thriving in this AI-powered era aren't necessarily the most tech-savvy; they're curious, adaptable, and just a bit strategic—much like Bernie, who has figured out that he gets treats from me (bribes) by stealing my socks when I'm not looking.

## What This Book Will Do for You

Here's the truth: 75% of professionals already use AI at work, even if it's just Grammarly rescuing them from typos. Companies are no longer debating if AI should be adopted —they're asking why you're not already on board. You don't need a PhD in machine learning to use AI tools effectively. You need to know which tools work, how to use them effectively, and where they can have the most significant impact. This book is your practical, jargon-free guide.

## Opportunities and Risks: The AI Balancing Act

Alright, let's talk about the elephant in the chatroom: **AI is powerful, but it's also a little bit of a wildcard.**

On one hand, AI is like the dream assistant you've always wanted—tireless, extremely fast, and miraculously immune to burnout. It can generate reports in seconds, write a half-decent LinkedIn post before you've finished your coffee, and even analyze data with a level of detail that would take a human hours (or, let's be honest, days). It's your secret weapon for getting more done in less time.

But here's the flip side—**AI doesn't always know what it's talking about.** Sometimes, it confidently delivers completely wrong answers like a first-year intern who hasn't quite figured out that *making things up* is not the same as "taking initiative." Ever seen an AI generate a citation for a court case that never existed? A medical diagnosis that defies biology? A sales email that sounds like a robot trying to impersonate a human *who has never met another human*? Yeah, it happens.

So, while AI can be a game-changer, it also comes with **some serious caveats** that every professional needs to be aware of. Let's break it down.

**What AI Can Do for You (That You'll Love)**

1. **Eliminate the Grunt Work:** AI is brilliant at tackling repetitive, soul-draining tasks. Need to clean up a spreadsheet? Draft a client follow-up? Summarize a 50-page document in 30 seconds? AI has your back. It's the ultimate assistant—minus the need for coffee breaks or an annual bonus.
2. **Level the Playing Field:** In the past, innovative technology was something only the big players could afford. Now? Small business owners, freelancers, and solo professionals have access to AI tools that can rival the capabilities of Fortune 500 companies. AI-powered marketing, customer insights, and automation aren't just for tech giants anymore—they're available to *you* right now.
3. **Make You Look Like a Genius (Without the All-Nighters):** AI is a data powerhouse. It can analyze customer behavior, predict trends, and help you make informed decisions faster than any human team could. Need to personalize an email campaign? Optimize your LinkedIn posts for

engagement? Spot patterns in sales data? AI does in minutes what would typically take days of analysis—and you get to take all the credit.

4. **Give You More Time for What Matters:** Here's the real magic: AI doesn't replace creativity, strategy, or human connection—it frees you up for more of it. By automating mundane tasks, AI enables professionals to focus on high-impact work—the kind that drives meaningful change. Instead of wasting time on admin tasks, you can focus on closing deals, brainstorming your next viral campaign, or just leaving work at a reasonable hour for once.

**Where AI Can Go Off the Rails (And Why You Need to Stay in the Driver's Seat)**

1. **The Confidence of a Used Car Salesman (With Half the Accuracy):** AI is *incredibly* confident. It will generate answers with unwavering certainty, even when it's completely wrong. This is what's known as "AI hallucination" (which sounds way cooler than it is). Suppose you trust AI outputs without verifying them. In that case, you're setting yourself up for some very awkward moments—especially in fields like law, healthcare, or finance, where **"close enough" is not a valid strategy.**
2. **Garbage In, Garbage Out:** AI isn't magic—it's only as good as the data it's trained on. If you feed it

flawed, biased, or outdated information, guess what? You'll get flawed, prejudiced, and obsolete results. This is particularly important in industries where accuracy is critical. AI can't fact-check itself, so *you* need to be the final filter between what it produces and what you use.

3. **The Ethical Landmines:** AI raises serious questions about data privacy, bias, and job displacement. If AI is automating tasks that once required humans, what happens to those jobs? If AI models are trained on biased data, how do we ensure fair outcomes? And if you're using AI for sensitive work, where is your data going? These are genuine concerns, and ignoring them isn't an option. Professionals who use AI responsibly—understanding both its power and its pitfalls—will be the ones who thrive in this evolving landscape.
4. **The Risk of AI Over-Reliance:** AI is a tool, not a replacement for critical thinking. The moment you rely on AI to make all your decisions for you, you've crossed into dangerous territory. AI should *augment* your expertise, not replace it. Think of it like GPS—successful for navigation, but if you mindlessly follow it without question, you might end up driving into a lake.

### How to Stay on the Right Side of the AI Revolution

AI is neither a miracle cure nor a doomsday device—it's a tool. And like any tool, it can be used brilliantly or disastrously, depending on how well you understand it. The key is learning to use AI strategically, knowing when to trust it and when to double-check its work.

In this book, you'll learn exactly how to leverage AI without losing control, so you can maximize efficiency without falling into the pitfalls. Each chapter will break down AI's best applications in different industries, with step-by-step guides on using it effectively—*without ending up in an AI-fueled disaster scenario.*

Because AI won't replace professionals, but professionals who use AI will replace those who don't.

So, if you're ready to work smarter, avoid AI's pitfalls, and use it as a force multiplier in your career, let's keep going.

**How to Use This Book**

Alright, you've made it this far, which means two things:

1. You're curious enough about AI to want to use it instead of just nodding along in meetings while your coworkers throw around terms like "machine learning" and "neural networks."
2. You don't have time for fluff. You need practical, actionable AI strategies that will help you in your industry—right now.

Good news: This book is **a hands-on guide,** not a theoretical deep dive that makes your eyes glaze over. You won't find lengthy discussions about AI ethics or the philosophical implications of sentient robots (although, if AI starts developing opinions about pineapple on pizza, we'll revisit that). What you *will* find are real-world applications, **step-by-step guides, and the best AI tools for your profession.**

**Find What You Need, When You Need It**

I get it. You're busy. You don't have to read 300 pages before you can start implementing AI into your workflow. That's why I structured the book **so you can jump to the sections that matter most to you.**

- **If you're a marketer** drowning in content creation, ad targeting, and social media engagement, flip to the **Marketing** chapter and start using AI to scale your work.
- **If you're in sales**, constantly prospecting and writing cold emails—head straight to the **Sales** chapter and discover how AI can help you close more deals with less effort.
- **If you're a lawyer**, spending your life buried under contracts and legal research—skip to the **Law** chapter to see how AI can speed up your workflow while keeping your ethical obligations intact.
- **If you're in healthcare**, balancing patient care with endless documentation—go to the **Healthcare** chapter to see how AI is reducing burnout and improving diagnostics.

- **If you're an educator**, tired of grading and lesson planning—jump to the **Education** chapter and learn how AI can make your teaching life easier.
- **If you're a small business owner**, wearing too many hats at once, turn to the **Small Business** chapter to automate your operations, marketing, and customer service. And so on.

Each chapter is designed to **stand alone**, meaning you don't need to read this book cover to cover (unless you love my writing, in which case, I appreciate you). Identify your industry, review the tools and guides, and begin implementing.

**What You'll Get in Each Chapter**

Every industry-specific chapter follows a structured format to make things simple, practical, and immediately applicable. Here's what you can expect:

- A Quick Overview of AI in Your Industry.
- **No fluff, no technical jargon.** Just a quick reality check on how AI is already transforming your field.
- The **Best AI Tools** for Your Work. A curated list of AI tools that work for your job. Not every AI tool is created equal—this book filters out the gimmicks and highlights only the best tools, with pros, cons, and real-world use cases.
- **Step-by-Step How-To Guides.**

- You won't just get a list of tools—you'll get **clear, no-nonsense walkthroughs** on how to use them. Whether it's setting up an AI-powered email campaign, analyzing contracts with AI, or using AI to draft LinkedIn posts, you'll get real instructions you can follow today.
- <u>Best Practices & Common Mistakes to Avoid</u>
- AI is powerful, but it can also go horribly wrong if misused. Each chapter includes the **do's and don'ts of AI in your profession** so you don't accidentally create AI-generated chaos (or worse, lose credibility with your clients and colleagues).
- **Future Trends** & How to Stay Ahead.
- Each chapter ends with a **look ahead at what's coming,** so you're not just keeping up—you're staying ahead of the curve.

**How to Get the Most Out of This Book**

- Start With What Applies to You.
- Don't feel pressured to read everything at once. Go straight to the chapter that applies to your work, and start implementing AI into your daily routine. The real magic happens when you try the tools. Each chapter includes a hands-on tutorial—do it as you read so you can see the impact for yourself.
- Experiment & Customize.
- The AI strategies in this book are a starting point. Tweak and adapt them to fit your unique

workflow. The more you experiment, the more valuable AI becomes.

- Don't Trust AI Blindly.
- AI is like a supercharged assistant, but it's not perfect. Always double-check AI-generated content, results, and recommendations—especially in high-stakes fields like law, healthcare, or finance.
- Keep Learning & stay updated. Once you've mastered the basics, continue to explore. New tools and updates roll out constantly, and the best professionals are the ones who stay ahead of the AI curve.

**Final Thought: This Book is Your AI Playbook—Use It**

This isn't a book you read once and forget. It's a guide you can refer to again and again, updating your skills as AI continues to evolve. The goal here isn't to overwhelm you with AI theory—it's giving you the exact tools, techniques, and strategies to use AI to your advantage, right now.

So go ahead—flip to your chapter, dive into the guides, and start making AI work for you.

Because one thing is certain: AI isn't going away. And professionals who know how to use it will be the ones leading the future.

# THE AI-POWERED LINKEDIN PLAYBOOK:

AUTOMATE CONNECTIONS, BUILD AUTHORITY, AND GENERATE LEADS

## The New Frontier of LinkedIn Outreach: Beyond Manual Connection Requests

For years, the playbook for LinkedIn outreach was simple, straightforward, and soul-crushingly manual. You would spend hours searching for prospects, meticulously crafting a connection request you hoped was just the right blend of professional and personable, and then, if accepted, you'd follow up with a pitch. This "Connect and Pitch" model was a numbers game played on foot. The professional who put in the most hours clicking, typing, and tracking their interactions in a sprawling spreadsheet was the one who won.

That era is officially over.

Welcome to the new frontier of professional outreach, a landscape being reshaped by AI. We are transitioning from a manual effort model to one of intelligent automation. The goal is no longer to connect; it's to **connect and converse at scale.**

Imagine this: Instead of spending your Monday morning searching for 50 prospects, an AI system identifies 500 ideal prospects for you while you sleep. Instead of sending a generic connection request, your AI assistant references a post your prospect wrote just this morning, drafts a thoughtful connection message, and schedules it to be sent at the exact time they are most likely to be active. And once connected, it doesn't just pitch; it starts a multi-step sequence of valuable insights, relevant questions, and helpful resources, all personalized to that individual's role and industry.

This isn't science fiction. This is the reality of using AI on LinkedIn today. These tools are not about replacing the human element of your work; they are about amplifying it. They handle 80% of the repetitive and process-driven outreach—the searching, clicking, scheduling, and basic follow-ups—so you can dedicate your uniquely human skills to the 20% that truly matters: building relationships, solving complex problems, and closing deals.

The core principle of this new playbook is simple: **Automate the process, not the personality.** We are not creating an army of spam bots to bombard the platform with generic sales pitches. We are building a sophisticated, semi-autonomous system that enables you to appear in more places, with greater relevance, than was ever manually possible. It's about leveraging technology to amplify the very qualities that make you exceptional: your expertise, your voice, and your capacity to forge meaningful professional connections.

### Ethical Checkpoint #1: The Responsibility of Power

Before we dive into the "how," we must address the "how not to." These AI tools are incredibly powerful, and with that power comes a significant responsibility. The line between "intelligent, personalized outreach" and "creepy, automated spam" is thinner than you might think, and crossing it can have severe consequences.

- **Reputational Damage:** A poorly executed AI campaign can make you or your company look foolish, out of touch, or worse, deceptive. A single automated comment that completely misses the context of a sensitive post can undo months of careful brand-building.

- **Account Suspension:** LinkedIn is actively working to maintain the integrity of its platform. It has implemented sophisticated algorithms to detect and restrict accounts that exhibit bot-like behavior. Using these tools recklessly is the fastest way to get your account flagged, limited, or even permanently suspended. LinkedIn explicitly prohibits bots, crawlers, and auto-connect tools. Violations can lead to restrictions or bans. See the LinkedIn User Agreement.

To navigate this unfamiliar landscape successfully, you must adopt a foundational ethical filter for every action you automate. Before building any campaign or sequence, ask yourself this simple question:

> **"If I were the one receiving this message, would I feel respected and valued, or would I feel targeted and spammed?"**

This is the "Recipient's Rule." If the outreach would make *you* roll your eyes, feel intrusive, or prompt you to immediately reach for the "report" button, you are on the wrong track.

The goal is to use AI to be more human, not less. It's a tool to help you listen better, engage more thoughtfully, and offer value more consistently. Throughout this chapter, we will revisit this ethical checkpoint, developing strategies that are not only effective but also respectful, transparent, and designed to foster long-term trust—the only currency that truly matters in the world of professional relationships. With this principle as our guide, let's explore the tools that make this new frontier possible.

## The LinkedIn Automation Toolkit: A Deep Dive into the Modern Tools

Welcome to the arsenal. The tools detailed in this section are the engines that will power your AI-driven outreach strategy. It's crucial to understand that there is no single "best" tool; instead, there is only the tool that is best for *your specific goal.* Some are all-in-one powerhouses, while others are specialists designed to excel at a single task.

We will analyze each tool through a consistent framework, examining its core features, strengths and weaknesses, cost, and ideal use case.

**Compliance Spotlight:**
**LinkedIn Automation**
LinkedIn's **User Agreement** prohibits bots, crawlers, browser extensions, or third-party tools that auto-connect, scrape profiles, or mass-message on your behalf. Accounts caught using them risk **temporary restrictions** or even **permanent bans.**

**Safe Uses:** drafting personalized messages, brainstorming post ideas, and summarizing leads (before pasting them into LinkedIn yourself).
**Risky Uses:** auto-sending invitations, scraping profile data, running bots to like/comment at scale.
Think of it like LinkedIn's version of airport security: bring your own bag; don't let a robot carry it for you.
📖 Policies: LinkedIn User Agreement | Help: Automated Activity

**1. Powerin**

**Tool Profile:** Powerin is not a traditional outreach automation tool. It is a specialist, laser-focused on one of the most critical and often overlooked aspects of LinkedIn strategy:

**AI-powered engagement.** Its primary function is to help you build authority and warm up prospects by leaving intelligent, relevant comments on their posts, positioning you as a thoughtful expert in your field before you ever send a connection request.

**Key Features:**

- **AI-Generated Comments:** This is Powerin's crown jewel. The tool analyzes the content of a LinkedIn post (text, images, and even video context) and generates multiple comment suggestions. You can select a tone (e.g., "Insightful," "Question," "Supportive") to guide the AI.

- **Content Curation** provides a curated feed of posts from prospects you've designated, allowing you to efficiently engage with the most relevant content without the need for endless scrolling.
- **One-Click Engagement:** Once you select and approve a comment, you can post it directly from the Powerin interface.

**Positives (The "Pros"):**

- **High-Quality AI:** The comment-generating AI is remarkably sophisticated, often producing insights that are genuinely difficult to distinguish from those of a human.
- **Builds "Social Proof":** It excels at the "top-of-funnel" activity of establishing your brand as a familiar and respected name in your prospects' networks.
- **Safe Engagement Model:** Because it focuses on public engagement rather than direct messaging automation, its usage is less risky in the eyes of LinkedIn's algorithms.

**Negatives (The "Cons"):**

- **Niche Focus:** It is not an all-in-one solution. It does not send connection requests or automated message sequences. You will need other tools for that.
- **Requires Human Oversight:** This is also a positive because it will keep you from sending out posts without editing. You still need to read the post and select the best comment. Mindlessly posting AI-generated comments is a recipe for disaster.

**Cost Structure:** Typically operates on a subscription model, often with different tiers based on the number of comments that can be generated per month. Expect prices to range from approximately **$40 to $100 per month.**

**Best Use Case:** For consultants, coaches, and high-ticket B2B salespeople who need to establish themselves as thought leaders. It's the perfect tool for the first phase of any outreach strategy: warming up the audience.

### 2. Closely

**Tool Profile:** Closely is an all-in-one LinkedIn automation platform designed to cover the entire outreach funnel, from lead discovery to multi-step messaging. It combines a lead database with powerful automation sequences, making it a strong contender for teams that want a single, unified solution.

. . .

**Key Features:**

- **Automated Sequences:** Send connection requests, InMails, emails, and follow-up messages in a pre-defined sequence.
- **Built-in Lead Database:** Access to a B2B database to find prospects, which can then be directly imported into your outreach campaigns.
- **AI-Tailored Messaging:** The AI can help you write and personalize messages based on profile data.
- **Inbox Management:** Provides a unified inbox to manage all your LinkedIn conversations in one place, which is more efficient than the native LinkedIn inbox.

**Positives (The "Pros"):**

- **All-in-One Convenience:** This is both a positive and a negative. If you are lazy, you might be tempted to use all the automation features, which would violate LinkedIn's User Agreement. However, it is nice to have a lead database and automation tools in the same platform, streamlining the workflow significantly.
- **User-Friendly Interface:** The platform is intuitive and easier to learn than some of its more complex competitors.

- **Data Enrichment:** Can often find and verify prospect email addresses, enabling multi-channel outreach (LinkedIn + Email).

**Negatives (The "Cons"):**

- **Database Quality Varies:** Like any B2B database, the accuracy of the contact information can be inconsistent.
- **Less Granular Control:** Compared to a specialist tool like Dripify, it may offer fewer options for creating highly complex, conditional outreach funnels.
- **Cost Structure:** Subscription-based, with pricing typically starting around **$50 per month** for a basic plan and scaling up based on the number of credits used for database access and features.

**Best Use Case:** For sales teams and individuals who want a straightforward, powerful, all-in-one system for finding and engaging leads with no need to patch together multiple different tools.

**3. Dripify**

**Tool Profile:** Dripify is the choice for the serious automation strategist. It is renowned for its visual campaign builder, which allows users to create intricate, flowchart-style outreach campaigns. It treats LinkedIn as a full-fledged marketing funnel, providing the tools to control every step of the journey.

**Key Features:**

- **Visual Funnel Builder:** Drag-and-drop actions (e.g., "View Profile," "Send Connection Request," "Like Post," "Send Message") and set delays and conditions to create truly dynamic sequences.
- **Team Management & Analytics:** Excellent features for managing multiple team members' accounts, assigning roles, and analyzing performance with detailed reports.
- **Safety Mechanisms:** Advanced settings to mimic human behavior, including randomized delays, activity control, and smart limits to stay under LinkedIn's radar.

**Positives (The "Pros"):**

- **Unmatched Control & Flexibility:** The visual builder enables nearly limitless creativity in designing your outreach funnels.
- **Robust Analytics:** Provides deep insights into every step of your campaign, helping you identify and fix bottlenecks.
- **Excellent for Teams:** The collaboration and safety

features make it a top choice for agencies or sales teams managing multiple accounts.

**Negatives (The "Cons"):**

- **Steep Learning Curve:** It's tough to learn at first with all the choices. It requires a strategic mindset to use effectively.
- **Can Be Overkill for Simple Needs:** If all you want to do is send a simple connection-and-follow-up sequence, Dripify might be more tool than you need.
- **Cost Structure:** Offers several subscription tiers ranging from **$60 to $100 per month per user**, with higher tiers unlocking more advanced features and higher limits.

**Best Use Case:** For marketing agencies, sophisticated sales teams, and anyone who loves data and wants granular control over their automated outreach funnels.

### 4. Crystal Knows

**Tool Profile:** Crystal is a unique and powerful tool that brings personality insights into the sales process. It uses AI to analyze a person's public data (including their LinkedIn profile) to predict their DISC personality type. This allows you to tailor your communication style to what is most likely to resonate with them.

. . .

**Key Features:**

**Personality Analysis:** Provides a detailed report on a prospect's communication style, motivations, and even what words to use or avoid.

**Real-time Writing Assistant:** A browser extension provides suggestions on how to phrase your emails, InMails, and messages to match the recipient's personality.

**Meeting Playbooks:** Offers guidance on how to conduct meetings with different personality types.

**Positives (The "Pros"):**

- **A True "Superpower":** It provides a layer of insight that feels like a competitive advantage, helping you build rapport much faster.
- **Reduces Communication Friction:** Helps you avoid common communication missteps by adapting your natural style.
- **Practical, Actionable Advice:** The suggestions are not vague; they are specific and easy to implement immediately.

**Negatives (The "Cons"):**

- **It's an Educated Guess:** While impressively

accurate, the analysis is still a prediction. It's a guide, not a gospel.

- **Requires a Skillful User:** The information is only helpful if you take the time to understand and apply it. It requires a higher level of emotional intelligence from the user.
- **Cost Structure:** Offers a limited free version. Premium plans for individuals and teams can range from **$50 to $150 per month**, making it a significant investment.

**Best Use Case:** For enterprise sales reps, account managers, and anyone in a role where building deep, long-term relationships is critical. It's the ultimate tool for personalizing the *substance* and *style* of your communication, not just the data points.

### 5. AI-Powered Video Personalization (e.g., BHuman, Synthesia)

**Tool Profile:** This category of tools enables one of the most powerful outreach strategies available today: personalized video at scale. These platforms use AI to take a template video you record and then automatically customize it for hundreds or thousands of prospects, often by dynamically changing a name on a whiteboard, a website on a screen, or even using a synthetic version of your voice.

. . .

**Key Features:**

- **Dynamic Variables:** You can insert variables (like {{first_name}} or {{company_name}}) into your video script or visual elements.
- **AI Avatars & Voice Cloning (Synthesia):** Create a digital version of yourself to generate videos without ever stepping in front of a camera.
- **Real-Person Templates (BHuman):** Record one video, and the AI will seamlessly edit it to include personalized elements for each recipient.

**Positives (The "Pros"):**

- **Extremely High Engagement:** A personalized video stands out in a crowded inbox and can generate reply rates that are orders of magnitude higher than text-based outreach.
- **Builds Instant Connection:** It allows the prospect to see and hear you, creating a human connection before you've ever spoken.
- **Scalable "Wow" Factor:** It delivers a highly personalized experience that was previously impossible to scale.

**Negatives (The "Cons"):**

- **Can Be Costly:** These platforms often charge per

video generated, so that costs can add up quickly for large campaigns.

- **Requires Upfront Effort:** You need to script and record a high-quality template video, which takes more effort than writing an email.
- **The "Uncanny Valley":** With fully synthetic avatars, there's a risk the video can feel slightly unnatural or "off" if not produced carefully.
- **Cost Structure:** Highly variable. Some platforms charge a monthly subscription (e.g., **$50-$300/month**) that includes a certain number of video credits, with overage fees.

**Best Use Case:** For anyone looking to make a significant impact on high-value prospects. It's perfect for breaking into a new account, re-engaging a cold lead, or making a memorable impression in any B2B sales or networking context.

🛠 **Tool Spotlight: Synthesia**
Turns text into AI-generated training videos with avatars and voiceovers in multiple languages.
Learn more: synthesia.io

### The Strategic Playbook: How to Best Utilize Your AI Toolkit

Having the right tools is only half the battle. A powerful toolkit without a smart strategy is like a sports car without a driver—full of potential but going nowhere. This section provides the playbook. It breaks down a modern LinkedIn outreach campaign into three distinct phases, showing you exactly how and when to deploy your AI tools to move a prospect from a stranger to an engaged lead.

This isn't a rigid, one-size-fits-all formula. It's a flexible framework. Depending on your industry and goals, you might spend more time in one phase than another, but the underlying principles of **Engage, Personalize, and Nurture** remain constant.

### Phase 1: Building Authority with AI-Powered Engagement (The "Warm-Up")

**The Goal:** To become a familiar, respected, and welcome presence in your prospect's professional life *before* you ever ask for anything. The objective here is not to sell, but to establish credibility and "social proof." When your connection request finally arrives, you want their reaction to be, "Oh, it's them—they always have smart things to say," not, "Who is this person?"

**The Strategy:** This phase is all about adding value to the public conversation. We will use AI to do this consistently and at scale.

1. **Identify Your "Top 20" Prospects:** Start by identifying 20 key decision-makers or influencers

in your target space. These are your initial targets for deep engagement.

2. **Deploy Your AI Engagement Tool:** Use a tool like **Powerin** to create a dedicated feed for these 20 individuals. This is your daily "engagement dashboard."
3. **Establish a Daily "Commenting Cadence":** Commit to leaving 5-10 high-quality comments each day. The AI will handle the heavy lifting of generating content, but your role is to serve as the human editor.
4. **Mastering the "Comment Prompting" Framework:** Don't just accept the AI's first suggestion. Guide it. Use the tone selector to match the context of the post.
   - If the post is a question, use the "Insightful" or "Experience" tone to provide a valuable answer.
   - If the post is a strong statement, use the "Question" tone to challenge or add nuance respectfully.
   - If the post announces a success, use the "Supportive" tone, but add a specific detail the AI noticed (e.g., "Congrats on the launch! The new UI looks incredibly clean.").
5. **The Human Touch:** Your most critical role here is quality control. Before posting, ask: Does this comment add to the conversation? Is it relevant? Does it sound like me? A quick edit to inject your

unique voice or a personal anecdote can turn a good AI comment into a great one.

**Case Study: "The Consultant's Content Play"**

Sarah, a management consultant, wanted to land a contract with a major logistics firm. Instead of sending cold InMails to the COO, she added the COO and five of their direct reports to her Powerin feed. For three weeks, she spent 15 minutes each morning using the AI to help her craft insightful comments on their posts about supply chain optimization and team management.

When she finally sent a connection request to the COO, the message wasn't cold. It was: "Hi John, I've really been enjoying your team's posts on last-mile delivery challenges. Your take on drone implementation was particularly sharp. Would be great to connect."

The COO accepted within an hour and replied, "Thanks, Sarah. Your comments have been great. Glad to connect." The sales cycle was already warm before it even began.

**Phase 2: The Personalized First Touch (The "Connection")**

**The Goal:** To achieve a near-perfect connection acceptance rate and make a first impression so memorable that it demands a response. This marks the transition from public engagement to a direct, one-to-one request.

**The Strategy:** We will use AI to find the perfect "hook" for our connection request, tailoring the message so it feels like it was handcrafted for a single recipient.

1. **Choose Your Automation Engine:**
   - Select a tool like **Closely** or **Expandi** to manage the connection request sequence.
2. **The "Hook" Hierarchy:** Program your AI to find the most powerful personalization point available for each prospect, in this order:
   - **Hook #1 (Best): Recent Post.** "Hi Jane, just read your post on the future of AI in marketing. Your point about data privacy resonated, and I wanted to connect."
   - **Hook #2 (Good): Shared Connection.** "Hi Mark, I see we're both connected to John Smith. I've always respected his work at Acme Corp and, seeing your profile, wanted to reach out."
   - **Hook #3 (Standard): Profile Detail.** "Hi Emily, I was impressed by your background in transitioning from finance to a tech leadership

role. As someone in the industry, I'd love to connect."

3. **Integrate Personality Insights:**
    - Before launching your campaign, run your prospect list through **Crystal Knows.**
        - Add a custom field to your outreach tool with a key personality trait (e.g., "Direct," "Harmonious," "Analytical").
            - Use this to tweak the tone of your request subtly.
                - For a "Direct" personality, keep it short and to the point.
                - For a "Harmonious" one, mention a shared connection to build trust.
4. **The Personalized Video Gambit:** For your absolute top-tier prospects, this is the ultimate move.
    - **Step A:** Record a 30-second template video using a tool like **BHuman.**
        - Stand in front of a small whiteboard. The script is simple: "Hi {{first_name}}, I saw your work at {{company_name}} and recorded this short video with a thought I had."
    - **Step B:** Upload your prospect list. The AI will generate a unique video for each person, with their name and company appearing on the whiteboard.

- **Step C:** In your connection request message, include a link to the video. The novelty and high level of personalization make it almost impossible to ignore.

**Phase 3: Automating the Follow-Up (The "Nurture")**

**The Goal:** To stay top-of-mind and build the relationship after the connection is made, all without lifting a finger. The key is to provide consistent value, rather than sending annoying reminders.

**The Strategy:** We will design a multi-step, multi-channel follow-up sequence that feels less like a sales pitch and more like a helpful conversation with a trusted expert.

1. **Design Your "Value-First" Sequence:** Using a tool like **Dripify** or **HeyReach**, map out a sequence that spans 2-3 weeks.
   - **Day 1 (Post-Connection):** Thank You & Context. "Great to connect, {{first_name}}. As I mentioned, I was interested in your thoughts on [topic]. No pitch here, just wanted to share an article I found on the subject that you might find interesting. [Link]."
   - **Day 4: Engage with Content.** The AI action is not to send a message, but to **like or comment**

**on their most recent post**. This keeps you on their radar in a non-intrusive way.

- **Day 9: The "Helpful Resource."** "Hi {{first_name}}, my team just published a case study on how a company like {{company_name}} solved [problem]. Thought you might find the results on page 4 particularly relevant. Happy to discuss if it sparks any ideas."
- **Day 15: The "Ask."** Only now, after providing value multiple times, do you make a soft ask. "Hi {{first_name}}, based on our shared interest in [topic], I'm curious to learn how you're handling [challenge] at {{company_name}}. Would you be open to a brief 15-minute chat next week to exchange ideas?"

2. **Implement the "Human Intervention" Rule:** This is the most critical ethical checkpoint of this phase.
    - **Set the Trigger:** Configure your automation tool to **immediately pause all future automated messages for a prospect the moment they reply.**
    - **Take the Wheel:** Once a prospect responds, it's your turn. The AI has successfully opened the door; *now it's your job to step through it and have a genuine, human conversation.* This single rule prevents the embarrassing mistake of an

automated message being sent right after a prospect has asked you a specific question.

### Measuring Success and Avoiding Pitfalls

An AI-powered outreach campaign is not a "set it and forget it" machine. It is a dynamic system that requires monitoring, refinement, and a keen awareness of the potential pitfalls. The most successful practitioners are not just good at setting up campaigns; they are experts at analyzing the results and making intelligent adjustments. This last section will provide you with the framework for measuring your success and the wisdom to avoid the most common—and costly—mistakes.

### Key Metrics to Track: Moving Beyond Vanity Numbers

To understand if your strategy is truly working, you need to track the correct data. Looking at the number of messages sent is a vanity metric; it tells you the machine is running, but not if it's getting you anywhere. Engagement and conversion, not just activity, measure a successful campaign.

Here are the essential metrics to build your performance dashboard around:

1. **Connection Acceptance Rate: What it is:** The percentage of connection requests that are

accepted. (Accepted Connections / Total Requests Sent) * 100.

- **Why it matters:** This is the gateway metric. A low acceptance rate (typically below 20-30%) is a red flag that your targeting is off, your connection message is weak, or you haven't sufficiently warmed up your prospects.
- **Goal:** Aim for **40% or higher**. A high acceptance rate shows your personalization and authority-building efforts are effective.

2. **Positive Reply Rate:**
   - **What it is:** The percentage of prospects who reply to your follow-up messages with a positive or neutral response. This explicitly excludes negative replies, such as "Not interested" or "Unsubscribe."
   - **Why it matters:** This is arguably the most critical metric. It measures genuine engagement. A high reply rate shows that your messaging is resonating and providing value, effectively opening the door to an authentic conversation.
   - **Goal:** This varies by industry, but a **10-15% positive reply rate** on a cold sequence is a powerful signal of success.
3. **Meetings Booked / Leads Generated:**
   - **What it is:** The ultimate conversion metric. How many of your positive replies translate

into a scheduled meeting, a demo request, or a qualified lead passed to the sales team?
   - **Why it matters:** This measures the direct business impact of your campaign. It connects your outreach efforts to tangible revenue-generating activities.
   - **Goal:** This is highly dependent on your business model, but you should have a clear goal (e.g., "Generate five qualified meetings per week from this campaign").

4. **Profile Views:**
   - **What it is:** An increase in the number of people viewing your LinkedIn profile.
   - **Why it matters:** This is a secondary, but essential, health metric. It indicates that your engagement activities (like commenting) and outreach are making people curious enough to learn more about you. It's a sign of growing authority and brand awareness.
   - **Goal:** A steady, noticeable week-over-week increase in profile views from your target industry.

## Common Mistakes and How to Avoid Them

The power of AI automation comes with an equal potential for error. The mistakes made here are not minor typos; they can be campaign-killing, reputation-damaging blunders. Here are the most common pitfalls and how to proactively avoid them.

**Mistake #1: Over-automation and "Setting and Forgetting"**

- **The Pitfall:** You launch a campaign and don't check on it for a week. In that time, it sends an automated follow-up to a prospect who has already replied, or it sends a message that is now comically out of date due to a recent news event.
- **The Solution: The Daily Check-in.** Spend 10 minutes every morning reviewing your campaign's activity. Check the replies in your unified inbox. Pause the automation for anyone who has responded. This simple habit is the single most effective way to prevent embarrassing mistakes. **Remember: the AI's job is to start conversations, not to have them for you.**

**Mistake #2: Generic AI Prompts and Robotic Messaging**

- **The Pitfall:** You rely on the AI tool's default message templates or provide it with lazy, low-effort prompts. The result is outreach that sounds robotic and impersonal, defeating the entire purpose of using AI for personalization.
- **The Solution: Become a "Prompt Engineer."** Your results are a direct reflection of the quality of your instructions. Spend significant

time crafting your prompts and message templates. Inject your voice, your company's unique value proposition, and specific, value-driven language. Test different versions (A/B testing) to see which prompts yield the highest positive reply rate.

**Mistake #3: Ignoring LinkedIn's Rules and "Red Flags"**

- **The Pitfall:** To maximize volume, you set your automation tool to send hundreds of connection requests a day, far exceeding LinkedIn's informal limits (typically around 100-200 per week). Your account will be flagged, and your ability to send new connection requests will be suspended for a week or more.
- **The Solution: Prioritize Safety and Mimic Human Behavior.** Use the safety features built into tools like Dripify or Expandi. Set your daily limits well within a reasonable human range. Schedule your campaigns to run only during regular business hours. Use randomized delays between actions. It is always better to run a slightly slower, safer campaign that runs consistently than a hyper-aggressive one that gets your account shut down.

**Mistake #4: Crossing the "Creepy" Line with Personalization**

- **The Pitfall:** You use the AI to find and reference a piece of information that is too personal (e.g., a photo from a family vacation on their Instagram, a comment on a personal Facebook post). Your attempt at personalization comes across not as thoughtful but as invasive and unsettling.
- **The Solution: The "Public Professional" Rule.** As a strict guideline, only reference information that is publicly available on their **LinkedIn profile** or their **company's website.** This is the information they have curated for a professional context. Referencing a recent promotion, a post they wrote about their industry, or a project featured on their company blog is an innovative approach. Referencing their child's soccer game is not. When in doubt, always err on the side of being more professional and less personal.

## Case Study: Hyper-Personalization at a B2B SaaS Company

- **Company:** "InnovateLeads," a mid-size B2B SaaS company selling project management software to enterprise clients.
- **Challenge:** Their marketing was effective at generating broad awareness but struggled with converting high-value enterprise leads. Their

content was generic, and their ad campaigns had low engagement rates among C-suite executives. They needed to demonstrate their understanding of the specific, nuanced challenges faced by different enterprise verticals (e.g., construction, biotech, finance).

- **Advanced AI Implementation:** They adopted a multi-layered AI strategy focused on deep personalization.
    1. **AI-Powered Audience Segmentation:** They used **HubSpot's AI** to analyze their existing customer data and identify "micro-personas." Instead of just "Project Managers," the AI identified "Construction PMs concerned with on-site safety compliance" and "Biotech PMs focused on FDA approval timelines."
    2. **Dynamic Content Generation:** Using **Jasper AI** integrated with their product data, they created a repository of content snippets (case studies, feature benefits, testimonials) tagged by micro-persona. They then built a dynamic landing page that utilized AI to create a unique version for each visitor, tailored to their industry and browsing behavior. A visitor from a finance company would see content about "SEC compliance and audit trails," while a visitor from the construction industry would see content about "managing subcontractor timelines."

3. **Predictive Ad Targeting:** They fed their micro-persona data into **Meta's Advantage+** and **LinkedIn's Predictive Audiences** AI. Instead of targeting broad job titles, they targeted users who exhibited behaviors and interests aligned with their specific micro-personas, letting the ad platforms' AI find lookalike audiences with much higher precision.

- **Results:**
  - **Conversion Rate** on enterprise-targeted landing pages increased by **250%.**
  - **Ad Spend ROI** improved by **75%** by eliminating wasted spend on irrelevant audiences.
  - **Sales Cycle Shortened:** The sales team reported leads were "significantly more educated" and "already understood the value proposition for their specific industry," reducing the time from first contact to demo by an average of 12 days.
- **Key Takeaway:** Advanced AI marketing isn't just about creating one piece of content faster; it's about creating a dynamic, self-personalizing system that makes every potential customer feel you're speaking directly to them.

## LinkedIn Personal Branding for the AI-Powered Marketer

In a field as crowded as marketing, your brand is your ultimate differentiator. It's what makes a potential client, employer, or partner choose *you* over thousands of others with similar skills. AI is your secret weapon for building that brand with precision and consistency.

**Your Goal:** To be seen not just as a marketer, but as a forward-thinking strategist who understands the future of the industry.

### AI-Powered Plays for Your LinkedIn Brand:

### The "Trend Weaver" Post:

- ***The Play:*** *Use* ***Perplexity AI*** *or* ***Readwise*** *to synthesize the top 3-5 articles on an emerging marketing trend (e.g., "the death of third-party cookies," "the rise of nano-influencers"). Ask the AI:* "Summarize the key arguments and counterarguments from these articles. Identify one common thread and one major point of disagreement."
- ***Your Human Touch:*** *Don't just post the summary. Add your unique perspective. Start your LinkedIn post with a strong,*

*contrarian hook the AI helped you identify. For example:* "Everyone's talking about AI in marketing, but they're missing the real story: it's about to make
creativity more valuable, not less. Here's the data..." *This positions you as a thought leader, not just a reporter.*

**The "Micro-Case Study" Carousel:**

- ***The Play:*** *Use* ***ChatGPT*** *to turn one of your recent successful campaigns into a compelling narrative. Prompt it:* "I ran a campaign that increased conversion rates by 40% using personalized landing pages. Turn this into a 5-slide LinkedIn carousel script following the 'Problem-Agitate-Solution-Result-Call to Action' framework."
- ***Your Human Touch:*** *Use* ***Canva's AI*** *to design the carousel using your brand colors quickly. The key is to share your* process, *not just the results. This demonstrates your expertise and provides your audience with a tangible takeaway, building trust and authority.*

**The "Smart Commenter" Strategy:**

***The Play:*** *Use* ***Powerin*** *to leave insightful, AI-assisted comments on posts by CMOs and marketing VPs at your dream companies. This is not about generic "Great post!" comments. The AI helps you add value at scale.*

**Your Human Touch:** *Before accepting the AI's suggestion, add a personal touch or a follow-up question.* "This is a great point on brand authenticity. It reminds me of how [Your Company] addressed a similar challenge by focusing on user-generated content, which resulted in a 20% increase in engagement. Have you found UGC to be as effective?" *This creates a dialogue and showcases your experience.*

# AI FOR MARKETING AND ADVERTISING

*How AI is Revolutionizing Marketing (and Making Your Job Easier, If You Let It*

It was 11:47 p.m., and Dana—marketing manager, serial tab hoarder, and two coffees past her bedtime—was watching her fifth ChatGPT tutorial of the night. Her deadline? In nine hours. Her task? Write a punchy LinkedIn post about Q2 metrics that didn't sound like it came from a bored intern or, worse, a bot with a LinkedIn addiction. "Why does everyone else make this look easy?" she muttered, glancing at her blank Google Doc like it owed her money.

If this scene feels a little too familiar, welcome. You're among friends.

Marketing has always been a blend of creativity and data—a pinch of intuition mixed with careful analysis, plus a healthy dose of second-guessing. Enter AI, your new best friend, who doesn't just take the guesswork out of your campaigns but promises not to laugh when your brilliant idea completely bombs. Even Bernie, my ever-faithful Bernedoodle and unofficial chief morale officer, might nod in approval—if he weren't already asleep on top of my keyboard.

If you're still relying solely on gut instinct or experience, it's like letting Bernie choose your next social media strategy—sure, it might be fun, but the results could be questionable. AI tools empower marketers to generate content ideas instantly, target ads with precision, and predict campaign outcomes—all without the usual coffee-induced heart palpitations.

## THE NEW AGE OF AI MARKETING: WHAT'S CHANGING?

Gone are the days of painstakingly split-testing ads or spending hours debating why your perfectly crafted message bombed. AI platforms are rapidly transforming marketing from guesswork to precise, data-driven creativity:

## The New Age of AI Marketing: What's Changing?

### What AI Is Doing for Marketers Right Now

We're way past the phase of "dabbling" with AI tools. They're here, they're powerful, and if used wisely, they won't just make your job easier—they'll make your work better.

**Real-World Use Snapshots:**

- **Elena, 42, SaaS Sales Director:** Uses Gong's AI features to spot patterns in rep behavior. After flagging which reps skipped follow-ups, her team hit quota for the first time in six quarters.
- **Tariq, 28, Solo Brand Designer:** Feeds ChatGPT his brand's tone guide, then uses it to generate weekly Instagram captions in 10 minutes flat. "It's like cloning myself," he says, "but my clone meets deadlines."
- **Maya, 55, Nonprofit Director:** Uses Canva's AI content planner and ChatGPT to draft monthly donor emails and grant summaries. "We saved

enough time to start that community garden project, finally."

**Key Shifts AI Has Brought to Marketing:**

- **Content Creation on Command**–Tools like ChatGPT and Jasper are your new brainstorming buddies. Need ad copy, captions, or a blog opener? They've got you.
- **Hyper-personalization at scale—yes**, your emails might now know more about your customers than their therapists. Use responsibly.
- **Ad Optimization**—Google and Meta's AI features are now so sophisticated that your old Excel budget tracker might question its life choices.
- **SEO Tools with Superpowers**—No more keyword guesswork. AI tools like SurferSEO practically whisper sweet Google ranking secrets in your ear.
- **Real-Time Customer Insights**—Want to know what your audience will love *before* you hit "publish"? AI's got predictive analytics for that.

Sounds great, right? However, before you let AI write your entire content strategy, there's one big caveat: AI is only as good as the marketer using it. Just because AI *can* generate content doesn't mean it *should*—without human oversight, you risk producing generic, soulless copy that reads like it was written by an algorithm (because, well, it was).

AI is here to **assist you, not replace you**—and if you learn how to use it strategically, you'll be light-years ahead of marketers who are still doing everything manually.

### The Must-Have AI Tools for Marketers

With hundreds of AI marketing tools out there, the key is knowing which ones are useful and which ones are just hype. Below is a curated list of the most effective AI tools for different aspects of marketing, along with their best use cases and potential drawbacks.

### Content Creation & Copywriting

**ChatGPT (OpenAI)**—Great for brainstorming content ideas, drafting blog outlines, and generating short-form copy (social media posts, email subject lines, ad headlines).

> ***Best Use:*** *When you need a quick first draft.*
> ***Watch Out For:*** *AI-generated content can sound robotic. Always edit to add your brand's personality.*

**Jasper AI** – Designed for marketing copy, blog writing, and ad creation with built-in templates for different formats (Google Ads, Facebook Ads, email sequences).

***Best Use:*** *Marketers looking for structured AI assistance with copywriting.*
***Watch Out For:*** *Overuse can lead to generic, formulaic content.*

**Copy.ai** – AI-driven content generator specializing in high-converting ad copy, product descriptions, and social media captions.

***Best Use:*** *When you need quick, engaging marketing copy without starting from scratch.*
***Watch Out For:*** *Needs human tweaking to ensure originality and tone consistency.*

**SEO & Content Optimization**

**Surfer SEO**—AI-powered content analysis that suggests keyword usage, readability improvements, and structure tweaks to boost Google rankings.

***Best Use:*** *SEO-driven content strategies for blogs and websites.*
***Watch Out For:*** *Content should still sound human, not just keyword-packed.*

**MarketMuse** – AI-driven content planner that identifies gaps in your topic coverage and suggests improvements.

> ***Best Use:*** *When planning long-form content or pillar pages.*
> ***Watch Out For:*** *Can be overwhelming. Use selectively for deep dives.*

**AI for Paid Ads & Social Media**

**AdCreative.ai** – Automatically generates ad creatives, including copy and visuals, optimized for high engagement.

> ***Best Use:*** *Facebook and Instagram ad creatives.*
> ***Watch Out For:*** *AI-generated ads can still benefit from human creative input to ensure uniqueness.*

**Persado** – AI-powered emotional intelligence for marketing copy—analyzes customer emotions and tailors messaging accordingly.

> ***Best Use:*** *Personalized email campaigns and ad copywriting.*
> ***Watch Out For:*** *Needs strong data integration to be fully effective.*

**Taplio** – AI tool for LinkedIn content creation and scheduling, helping you stay visible in your industry.

**Best Use:** *Personal branding and thought leadership on LinkedIn.*
**Watch Out For:** *AI can generate posts, but genuine human interaction is still required for engagement.*

**Customer Insights & Analytics**

**HubSpot Smart CRM AI** – AI-driven insights into customer behavior, email engagement, and lead scoring.

**Best Use:** *Sales & marketing automation for mid-size businesses.*
**Watch Out For:** *Requires integration with CRM for maximum impact.*

**Zeta Global AI** – Uses machine learning to predict customer intent and optimize marketing campaigns.

**Best Use:** *Large-scale ad campaigns with deep customer segmentation.*
**Watch Out For:** *Works best with large datasets —not ideal for small businesses with limited customer data.*

**🛠 Tool Spotlight: Jasper**

An AI writing assistant built for marketing. Jasper helps

generate ad copy, social posts, and even complete campaign drafts.

Learn more: Jasper.ai

## Step-by-Step: Launching a Marketing Campaign with AI

Let's walk through what an actual AI-assisted campaign looks like. Spoiler: it doesn't involve sorcery, just innovative tools.

### Step 1: Ideation & Messaging

Use **ChatGPT** or **Jasper** to brainstorm ad themes or concise email introductions.

*Prompt Example:* "Write five headlines for a product launch about a solar-powered phone charger, target audience: outdoor lovers."

### Step 2: Visual & Copy Creation

Tools like **AdCreative.ai** take your product image and brand tone, then whip up high-performing ad variants faster than your intern can say "target audience."

### Step 3: Audience Targeting & Personalization

AI platforms like **Persado** help you craft emotionally resonant messages (without sounding like a Hallmark card), while **HubSpot AI** tailors emails by behavior and history.

**Step 4: SEO Tune-Up**

Run your landing page through **Surfer SEO** for keyword suggestions and structural tweaks. Suddenly, SEO doesn't feel like dark magic.

**Step 5: Analytics & Optimization**

Let **Google Ads AI** handle bid adjustments while **Zeta Global** surfaces which messages are converting—and why.

---

Now that you know which tools to use, let's put them into action. In this section, we'll walk through a real-world AI-powered marketing workflow—from content creation to ad targeting to optimization.

💡 **Scenario:** You're launching a new product and need to create a multi-channel marketing campaign. Here's how AI can streamline the process:

**Step 1: Generate Your Campaign Theme & Messaging**

- Use **ChatGPT** or **Jasper** to brainstorm taglines, ad copy, and content ideas for your campaign.

- Example prompt: *"Generate five compelling headlines for a social media campaign promoting a new eco-friendly water bottle."*

**Step 2: Create AI-Optimized Ad Creative**

- Use **AdCreative.ai** to generate ad visuals and copy based on your brand style.
- Example: Upload your product photo → AI creates different variations of Facebook ad creatives optimized for engagement.

**Step 3: Personalize & Optimize Your Messaging**

- Use **Persado** or **HubSpot AI** to personalize your messaging for different audience segments.
- Example: AI suggests using "curiosity-driven" copy for Gen Z and "social proof" messaging for millennials.

**Step 4: Optimize Your Ads & Content with AI Analytics**

- Let **Google Ads' AI** bidding system optimize your ad spend.
- Utilize Surfer SEO to refine your blog content for improved search engine rankings.

**Step 5: Track, Analyze, and Improve**

- AI-powered tools like **HubSpot** or **Zeta Global** will help you measure what's working—and what needs tweaking.

## Case Study: Proactive Retention at a Subscription Service

- **Company:** "ConnectSphere," a subscription-based networking platform for professionals.
- **Challenge:** The company was suffering from a high "silent churn" rate. Customers wouldn't complain; their usage would drop off over a few weeks, and they would fail to renew their annual subscription. The support team was reactive, dealing only with inbound complaints.
- **Advanced AI Implementation:** They built a "Proactive Retention Engine" using several integrated AI tools.
    - **AI-Powered Health Scoring:** Using **Salesforce Einstein AI**, they created a dynamic "Customer Health Score" for every user. The AI analyzed dozens of data points in real-time: login frequency, number of connections made, messages sent, profile completion percentage, and even help-desk ticket sentiment.
    - **Automated "Nudge" Sequences:** When a customer's health score dropped below a

certain threshold (e.g., from 90 to 70), it automatically triggered a personalized, non-intrusive "nudge" sequence via **Lavender.ai.** The AI would draft an email highlighting an underused feature relevant to their industry or inviting them to a webinar. The goal was to re-engage, not to sound an alarm.

  - **Conversation Intelligence for Churn Prediction:** They used **Gong.io** to analyze all customer support calls. The AI was trained to detect "churn-related keywords" and sentiment patterns (e.g., frustration, confusion about pricing, mentions of competitors). If these patterns were detected, the customer's health score was automatically lowered, and their account was flagged for a personal follow-up from a senior customer success manager.

- **Results:**
  - Reduced customer churn by **32%** within six months.
  - Increased customer engagement with "at-risk" features by **50%.**
  - Shifted the customer success team's focus from "reactive problem-solving" to "proactive value-creation," which significantly improved team morale and effectiveness.
- **Key Takeaway:** Advanced AI in sales isn't just for finding new customers; it's a powerful tool for

keeping the ones you have by understanding their behavior at a scale no human team could manage.

### Final Thoughts: AI Won't Replace Marketers, But Marketers Who Use AI Will Replace Those Who Don't

Marketing is evolving—fast. **AI won't make you obsolete,** but if you *don't* use it, you're voluntarily putting yourself at a disadvantage.

Start experimenting with AI marketing tools today—because **your competitors already are.**

# AI FOR SALES AND CUSTOMER RELATIONSHIP MANAGEMENT

*How to Sell Smarter, Close Faster, and Avoid the Soul-Crushing Tedium of Manual Follow-Ups*

SALES USED TO BE ABOUT CHARISMA, GUT INSTINCTS, AND possibly a little bit of black magic. The best salespeople could read a prospect like a poker pro at the World Series and knew precisely when to push, when to back off, and when to throw in an "I understand where you're coming from" for maximum persuasion.

But let's be real—modern sales isn't just about smooth talk anymore. It's about speed, efficiency, and personalization at scale. And that's where AI is turning good salespeople into *unstoppable selling machines.*

If you're still manually tracking leads, writing the same follow-up email 27 times, or spending hours trying to figure out why your pipeline suddenly looks like a desert wasteland—AI is here to save you. The best part? You don't have to be a tech wizard to use it. Just plug in the right tools, let AI do the heavy lifting, and focus on what you do best: **closing deals.**

## The Evolving Sales Stack with AI

Let's cut to the chase: AI isn't replacing salespeople—it's replacing salespeople who refuse to adapt.

The best sales teams aren't spending their time manually prospecting, sending cold emails from scratch, or wasting energy on leads that will never convert. They're using AI-powered tools that tell them who to contact, when to reach out, and what to say—before their competition even knows there's a deal to be made.

Here's what AI is doing for top-performing sales teams:

- **Lead Scoring on Autopilot** – AI analyzes past deal data to rank leads by likelihood to close. Instead of guessing, you'll know exactly which prospects deserve your time.
- **Predictive Sales Forecasting** – No more gut-feeling revenue projections. AI analyzes patterns and past sales cycles to tell you what's coming—before you even feel it.
- **Automated Follow-Ups** – AI-driven email sequences ensure that no lead falls through the cracks (because let's be honest, manual follow-ups are a nightmare).
- **Call & Meeting Intelligence** – AI records, transcribes, and analyzes your sales calls, highlighting the exact moments where your prospect showed buying intent—or started mentally checking out.
- **Sales Email Optimization** – AI can analyze past email data to tell you which subject lines get opened and which messages get responses. No more sending emails into the void.

If you're still doing sales the old-fashioned way, AI isn't your enemy—it's your golden ticket to an easier, more productive workflow. And if that means less time spent writing repetitive emails and more time closing deals, then why wouldn't you jump on board?

## The Best AI Tools for Sales Professionals

Alright, let's talk about the real moneymakers—the AI tools that will help you sell smarter and faster. Below are the top AI-powered sales tools, categorized by their primary strengths.

### AI-Powered CRM Assistants

**HubSpot Sales Hub AI** – AI-driven sales assistant that prioritizes leads, suggests email responses, and automates data entry (so you're not manually logging every call like it's 1999).

> ***Best Use:*** *Small-to mid-size businesses looking for an all-in-one sales automation tool.*
>
> ***Watch Out For:*** *Works best if your CRM is already well-organized—otherwise, it's like throwing AI into a messy closet and expecting it to sort your life out.*

**Salesforce Einstein AI** – The AI brain inside Salesforce Einstein that predicts which leads will convert, suggests next steps, and automates reporting.

> ***Best Use: Enterprise sales teams*** *who want AI-powered insights baked into their existing workflow.*
>
> ***Watch Out For:*** *Einstein is brilliant, but it's not free. Be ready for premium pricing.*

## AI for Lead Generation & Research

**ZoomInfo with Intent AI** – AI analyzes buyer behavior signals to tell you which leads are in-market and ready to buy.

> ***Best Use:*** *B2B sales teams who need high-quality, ready-to-close leads.*
> ***Watch Out For:*** *Works best with large datasets—if you're selling niche products, you might not get the volume you need.*

**Cognism** – an AI-powered prospecting tool that finds decision-makers' contact details (without the creepy factor of stalking them on LinkedIn).

> ***Best Use: Outbound sales teams*** *who want accurate, up-to-date contact info.*
> ***Watch Out For:*** *If you don't have a strong* ***outreach strategy****, Cognism is just handing you phone numbers you won't use.*

## AI for Sales Outreach & Email Personalization

**Lavender AI**—Analyzes your sales emails in real-time and suggests more persuasive language, better formatting, and even ideal send times.

> ***Best Use:*** *Salespeople who need to optimize email responses for better engagement.*

> ***Watch Out For:*** *Don't over-automate. AI can improve your email, but it still needs a human touch to sound authentic.*

**Regie.ai**—AI-powered email sequencing tool that writes and automates entire outreach campaigns.

> ***Best Use:*** ***Cold outreach campaigns*** *that need personalization at scale.*
> ***Watch Out For:*** *Generic AI-generated emails still need tweaking—you don't want your prospect receiving an email that sounds robotic.*

**AI for Call & Meeting Intelligence**

**Gong.io**—Records and analyzes sales calls, highlighting key buying signals, objections, and the best-performing talk tracks.

> ***Best Use:*** *Sales teams that do a lot of discovery calls and demos.*
> ***Watch Out For:*** *It will show you exactly where you're losing prospects—so be ready to face the truth.*

**Fireflies.ai**—AI-powered meeting assistant that transcribes sales calls and pulls out action items automatically.

> ***Best Use:*** *Reps who want to focus on the conversation instead of taking notes.*
> ***Watch Out For:*** *AI transcription isn't perfect—always review meeting summaries before sending.*

**AI for Sales Forecasting & Analytics**

**Clari AI** — an AI-driven forecasting tool that predicts deal outcomes based on pipeline activity.

> ***Best Use:*** *Sales leaders who need more accurate revenue forecasting.*
> ***Watch Out For:*** *Works best if your CRM data is clean and up to date.*

🛠 **Tool Spotlight: Apollo.io**
A sales intelligence platform with AI-driven prospecting, email sequencing, and analytics.
Learn more: Apollo.io

**Step-by-Step: Using AI to Close More Deals**

Now that you know which tools are worth your time, here's how you can use AI to transform your sales process from prospecting to closing.

**Scenario:** You need to identify, engage, and close high-value leads faster.

**Step 1: Identify Hot Prospects**

- Use **ZoomInfo Intent AI** to find leads that are already showing buying intent.
- Run those leads through **Salesforce Einstein AI,** which scores them by likelihood to convert.

**Step 2: Automate Personalized Outreach**

- Use **Regie.ai** to generate personalized email sequences tailored to each prospect.
- Optimize those emails with **Lavender AI** to improve open and reply rates.

**Step 3: Perfect Your Sales Calls**

- On discovery calls, use **Gong.io** to track prospect sentiment and refine your pitch.
- Let **Fireflies.ai** transcribe your meetings and suggest follow-up action items.

**Step 4: Close Faster & Forecast Smarter**

- Use **Clari AI** to track deals most likely to close this quarter.
- AI-driven analytics reveal where to focus efforts on pipeline gaps and enhance conversion rates.

## LinkedIn Personal Branding for the Elite Sales Professional

In sales, your brand is your reputation. A powerful brand precedes you, warming up cold calls and turning prospects into inbound leads. The modern sales professional doesn't just sell; they educate, advise, and build trust. AI is the key to doing this at scale, establishing you as a valuable resource, not just another vendor.

**Your Goal:** To be the first person a prospect thinks of when they have a problem you can solve, long before they are actively looking to buy.

### AI-Powered Plays for Your LinkedIn Brand:

**The "Problem-Solving" Framework Post:**

- ***The Play:*** *Think of the top 3-5 pain points your customers face. Use* **ChatGPT** *to turn one of them into a shareable framework.*
  *Prompt:* "My customers struggle with [specific problem]. Create a simple 4-step framework called 'The [Your Name/Brand] Method' that they can use to solve this problem. Write it as a concise, value-driven LinkedIn post."
- ***Your Human Touch:*** *Post this framework. Don't mention your product. The goal is to give*

*valuable advice for free. This builds reciprocity and positions you as a genuine expert. For example:* "Tired of messy sales pipelines? Try the 'Clarity Cascade' method: 1. Define Your Stages, 2. Set Exit Criteria, 3. Automate Data Entry, 4. Review Weekly. This simple process can save you 5 hours a week."

**The "Customer Hero" Story:**

***The Play:*** *Take a recent customer success story (with their permission and anonymized if necessary). Use* ***Claude*** *to write it as a compelling narrative.* *Prompt:* "Write a short LinkedIn story about a customer who was struggling with [problem] and used [our solution/approach] to achieve [result]. Focus on the customer as the hero of the story, not on our product features."

***Your Human Touch:*** *Share the story, tagging the customer's company if appropriate. This is far more powerful than a dry case study. It provides social proof and highlights the real-world impact of your work, building* *trust with prospects who have similar challenges.*

**The "Buying Signal" Engagement Strategy:**

***The Play:*** *Use LinkedIn Sales Navigator to identify prospects who have recently changed jobs or been promoted.*
*Use* ***Lavender.ai's*** *"Start My Email" feature to help you craft a congratulatory, non-salesy message. Prompt the AI to generate an opening line that is purely congratulatory and asks an open-ended question about their new role.*

***Your Human Touch:*** *Send the message. The key is to have zero sales pitches.* "Hi [Name], saw the news about your new role as Director at [Company]—congratulations! That's a fantastic move. I'm curious, what's the most exciting challenge you're tackling in the first 90 days?" *This starts a relationship based on genuine interest, not immediate need, and puts you on their radar at a critical buying moment.*

## Final Thoughts: AI Will Make You a Better Salesperson —If You Let It

The best salespeople aren't working harder; they're working smarter. AI isn't here to replace you—it's here to take the busywork off your plate so you can focus on what you do best: closing deals.

So stop manually tracking leads like it's 2005 and start using AI to sell faster, close smarter, and hit your numbers without burning out.

Your commission check will thank you.

# AI FOR CONTENT CREATION AND PERSONAL BRANDING

## *How to Write, Design, and Promote Like a Team of 10 (Without Actually Being a Team of 10)*

Once upon a time, content creation required actual time and effort—crafting blog posts from scratch, brainstorming social media captions over yet another cup of coffee, and staring blankly at a screen, hoping inspiration would strike before the deadline.

But welcome to the AI age, where content creators have access to an army of digital assistants who can write, design, edit, and even schedule posts while you sip your latte and take all the credit.

If you're still creating content the old-fashioned way, you're playing the game on hard mode. AI isn't here to replace your creativity—it's here to take the grunt work off your hands so you can focus on strategy, storytelling, and standing out.

So, whether you're a blogger, social media manager, video creator, or LinkedIn thought leader in the making, it's time to stop overworking and start automating.

## Content at Scale with AI – What's Changing?

There was a time when content marketing was a slow burn—weeks of planning, hours of writing, and a comprehensive strategy to launch a single campaign. Now? AI tools can generate blog posts, ad creatives, captions, and even complete video scripts in minutes.

### What AI Is Doing for Content Creators Right Now:

- **Generating Blog Posts & Articles in Minutes** – AI writing tools like **Jasper** and **ChatGPT** can draft entire articles with structured outlines, headers, and even SEO-friendly keywords.

- **Automating Social Media Posts** – AI tools can generate **hundreds of engaging post ideas,** complete with hashtags and captions that match your brand voice.
- **Creating Eye-Catching Visuals** – AI image generators like **DALL·E** and **Canva's AI tools** make designing content as easy as clicking a button.
- **Turning Text into Video Content** – AI-powered video tools
  like **Pictory** and **Synthesia** can transform blogs into short-form videos—perfect for TikTok, Instagram Reels, or LinkedIn.
- **Personalizing Content at Scale** – AI can analyze engagement data and help you tweak your content for maximum impact.

But Here's the Catch...

AI isn't perfect. It can generate a first draft, but it can't replace your voice, experience, or unique insights. The key to using AI successfully isn't letting it do all the work—it's using it to get 80% of the way there and adding the final 20% yourself.

Because let's be honest—if everyone uses AI-generated content without any human touch, we're all going to sound like clones of each other.

## The AI Tools Every Content Creator Needs

With so many AI tools available, how do you know which ones are truly useful? Below are the best-in-class AI tools for content creation, categorized by type.

### AI for Writing & Blogging

**ChatGPT (OpenAI)**—Your AI-powered writing assistant for brainstorming, drafting, and rewording content.

> ***Best Use:*** *When you need a quick article outline, blog post intro, or post ideas.*
> ***Watch Out For:*** *Don't copy-paste AI content as-is—it still needs editing to sound human.*

**Jasper AI**—AI-powered writing for marketing and branded content, with templates for emails, blogs, and ads.

> ***Best Use:*** *When you need structured, conversion-driven copy.*
> ***Watch Out For:*** *It's excellent for drafts, but weak on originality. Add your flair!*

**Copy.ai**—AI that writes ads, emails, and product descriptions in seconds.

***Best Use:*** *Quick-turnaround marketing copy that needs variety.*
***Watch Out For:*** *AI-generated copy can be generic. Always tweak for authenticity.*

**AI for Social Media & Personal Branding**

**Taplio**—AI-powered LinkedIn post generator, helping you craft engaging content without staring at a blank page.

***Best Use:*** *When you need consistent LinkedIn posts for thought leadership.*
***Watch Out For:*** *AI can generate ideas, but YOU bring the personality.*

**Hootsuite OwlyWriter AI**—Generates social media captions, post ideas, and content calendars.

***Best Use:*** *When you need bulk social media content across platforms.*
***Watch Out For:*** *AI isn't always brand-aware—review for consistency.*

**Lately.ai**—AI that analyzes past engagement data and generates social posts optimized for performance.

***Best Use:*** *For businesses repurposing content and automating engagement.*
***Watch Out For:*** *Needs high-quality data input to work effectively.*

## AI for Visual & Video Content

**Canva Magic Write & AI Image Generator**—AI-powered tools that create visuals, social posts, and branding elements in seconds.

> ***Best Use:*** *Quick-turnaround design when you don't have time for Photoshop.*
> ***Watch Out For:*** *AI-generated images; they might not match your brand style perfectly.*

**Pictory AI**—Turns blog posts into automated video summaries for social media.

> ***Best Use:*** *When you need short-form video content without filming anything.*
> ***Watch Out For:*** *AI-generated videos still need human editing for impact.*

**Synthesia AI**—AI-generated videos with realistic avatars and voiceovers.

> ***Best Use:*** *For professional, scalable video production (without hiring actors).*
> ***Watch Out For:*** *Overuse can feel robotic. Use wisely for business presentations.*

### Step-by-Step: Using AI to Produce a Week of Content

Let's get practical. **Here's a step-by-step guide** on how you can use AI to **batch-produce a week's worth of content.**

💡 **Scenario:** You need to plan, create, and schedule content across LinkedIn, Instagram, and your blog.

**Step 1: Generate Content Ideas**

- Use **ChatGPT** to brainstorm five content topics based on your niche.
- Example prompt: *"Give me five engaging content ideas about AI in marketing."*

**Step 2: Draft Your LinkedIn Posts**

- Use **Taplio** to create 3 LinkedIn post drafts—one thought leadership post, one engagement post, and one poll.
- Edit to match your brand voice and add personal insights.

**Step 3: Create Blog Content**

- Use **Jasper** to generate a structured blog post draft.
- Run it through **Surfer SEO** to optimize for search rankings.

### Step 4: Design Social Media Graphics

- Use **Canva AI** to create custom images for LinkedIn and Instagram.
- Use **DALL·E** to generate a unique visual concept for your campaign.

### Step 5: Automate Video Content

- Use **Pictory AI** to transform your blog post into a short-form video.
- Use **Synthesia** to create a talking-head video for LinkedIn.

### Step 6: Schedule & Publish

- Upload everything into **Hootsuite** and let AI suggest the best posting times.
- Sit back and enjoy your newfound free time.

## Final Thoughts: AI Won't Replace Your Creativity—It Will Amplify It

Great content still needs a human touch. AI can write, design, and optimize, but you bring the strategy, insights, and personality that make content truly stand out.

So don't be the person stuck manually writing captions and designing graphics from scratch while your competitors are batch-producing, automating, and scaling their brand.

Start using AI today and create smarter, not harder.

# AI FOR LAW

## SMARTER RESEARCH, FASTER CONTRACTS, AND FEWER ALL-NIGHTERS

### *Why AI Won't Replace Lawyers (But It Will Make You a More Efficient One)*

THE LEGAL PROFESSION HAS ALWAYS BEEN KNOWN for meticulous research, endless paperwork, and billing hours that make clients question their life choices. But what if AI could handle the drudgery, so lawyers could focus on strategy, argumentation, and, you know, actually practicing law?

If you're imagining a dystopian future where AI judges replace human ones—relax. The legal field isn't about to be overrun by robot attorneys (although some depositions would be a lot more entertaining if they were).

What AI *is* doing, however, is making lawyers faster, more efficient, and far less reliant on caffeine-fueled late nights. From automating contract analysis to predicting case outcomes to drafting legal documents in minutes instead of hours, AI is quietly revolutionizing the way law firms operate.

And if you're still doing legal work the old-fashioned way, your competitors are already outpacing you.

### The AI Revolution in Law: What's Changing?

For decades, legal research and case preparation have been slow, expensive, and mind-numbingly repetitive. AI is changing that overnight by handling tasks that used to take hours (or days) in minutes.

What AI is Doing for Lawyers Right Now:

- **Automating Legal Research** – AI-powered research tools scan millions of case files, precedents, and statutes in seconds—no more endless Westlaw rabbit holes.

- **Drafting Legal Documents in Minutes** – AI can generate contracts, NDAs, agreements, and demand letters with astonishing accuracy.
- **Analyzing and Summarizing Contracts** – Instead of manually combing through dense, 30-page contracts, AI tools can extract key clauses, flag risks, and compare contracts side by side.
- **Predicting Case Outcomes** – AI-powered litigation tools analyze past court decisions to forecast the likelihood of winning a case based on previous rulings and judge behavior.
- **Automating E-Discovery** – AI tools sift through thousands of documents in discovery to find relevant evidence, saving lawyers countless billable hours.

But Here's the Catch...

AI can analyze, summarize, and suggest, but it can't argue in court, exercise judgment, or think strategically. That's why AI won't replace lawyers—it will just give the best ones an unfair advantage.

Think of it like this: AI is the paralegal of the future—handling the grunt work so lawyers can spend more time strategizing and winning cases.

## The Best AI Tools for Lawyers

Law firms are increasingly adopting AI tools that boost efficiency, reduce research time, and eliminate tedious paperwork. Here are the top AI tools every modern lawyer should be aware of.

### AI for Legal Research & Case Law

**Casetext**—now part of Thomson Reuters - Casetext's CoCounsel is an AI-powered legal assistant that utilizes advanced AI to perform legal research, document review, deposition preparation, and contract analysis.

> ***Best Use:*** *Accelerating legal research by asking questions in natural language and getting direct, reliable answers with citations to the controlling authority.*
>
> ***Watch Out For:*** *As a premium, powerful tool, it represents a significant investment. Its deep integration works best for professionals already using the Thomson Reuters ecosystem.*

### AI for Contract Review & Drafting

**Evisort**—AI-powered contract analysis tool that identifies risks, extracts key clauses, and tracks compliance in legal agreements.

> ***Best Use:*** *Contract-heavy legal work that requires efficiency.*
> ***Watch Out For:*** *Works best for high-volume contract processing.*

**LawGeex**—an AI contract review platform that compares new agreements to your firm's standard clauses and flags inconsistencies.

> ***Best Use:*** *Reducing human error in contract analysis.*
> ***Watch Out For:*** *May miss subtle legal nuances that a trained attorney would notice.*

## AI for Litigation & Case Prediction

**Lex Machina**—an AI-powered litigation analytics tool that predicts case outcomes based on historical court rulings.

> ***Best Use:*** *Lawyers looking for data-driven insights on judges, opposing counsel, and case trends.*

***Watch Out For: Judges are human****—AI predictions aren't 100% foolproof.*

**Premonition AI**—Analyzes millions of court cases to determine which lawyers perform best before specific judges and the likelihood of success.

***Best Use:*** *Strategic litigation planning.*
***Watch Out For:*** *Data is useful, but not a guarantee of results.*

**AI for E-Discovery & Document Review**

**Relativity Trace**—AI-driven e-discovery platform that scans emails, files, and communications for relevant case information.

***Best Use:*** *Large-scale litigation and corporate investigations.*
***Watch Out For:*** *Works best when trained on case-specific data.*

**Everlaw**—an AI-powered document review and litigation support tool that categorizes and organizes legal files for easy retrieval.

***Best Use:*** *Reducing hours spent on document review.*

***Watch Out For:*** *Humans still need to verify findings.*

## Step-by-Step: Using AI to Automate Legal Work

Let's break it down into a real-world AI-powered legal workflow—from research to drafting to case analysis.

**Scenario:** You're a lawyer working on a breach of contract case. Here's how AI can streamline your workflow.

### Step 1: Find Relevant Case Law (Faster Than Ever)

- Use **Casetext CARA AI** to find similar breach of contract cases in seconds.
- AI suggests case law you might not have considered.

### Step 2: Review & Summarize Contracts Instantly

- Upload the disputed contract into **Evisort** or **LawGeex.**
- AI extracts key clauses, identifies risks, and compares them to past agreements.

### Step 3: Predict Case Outcomes & Strategy

- Run past rulings through **Lex Machina** or **Premonition AI** to analyze the judge's previous decisions in similar cases.

- AI suggests the likelihood of a settlement or trial win.

**Step 4: Automate Document Review in Discovery**

- Use **Relativity Trace** to scan thousands of client emails and documents for relevant case material.
- AI flags key evidence that could strengthen your argument.

**Step 5: Draft Legal Documents (Without Starting from Scratch)**

- Use a tool like **Casetext's CoCounsel** to generate a first draft of your legal brief or motion.
- AI automatically pulls in relevant statutes and case citations, providing a structured and well-supported starting point for your argument.

## LinkedIn Personal Branding for the Modern Lawyer

For lawyers, a personal brand on LinkedIn is about building trust and demonstrating expertise in a highly regulated and traditionally conservative field. It's not about flashy marketing; it's about projecting quiet confidence, deep knowledge, and a forward-looking perspective on the practice of law.

**Your Goal:** To be recognized as the go-to expert in your

specific niche (e.g., AI and intellectual property, data privacy law, M&A for tech startups).

**AI-Powered Plays for Your LinkedIn Brand:**

**The "Legal Explainer" Article:**

- ***The Play:*** *Use* ***Casetext's CoCounsel*** *or* ***Lexis+ AI*** *to research a complex new ruling or piece of legislation in your niche. Ask the AI:* "Summarize the key implications of the recent [Case Name] ruling for companies in the software industry. Explain it in plain English, avoiding legal jargon."
- ***Your Human Touch:*** *Publish this summary as a LinkedIn article. Your unique value is not just summarizing the law, but explaining its* business impact. *Start with a title like:* "The Supreme Court Just Changed Everything for SaaS Companies: Here's What You Need to Do Now." *This translates your legal expertise into practical business advice, attracting clients rather than just other lawyers.*

**The "Risk Radar" Post:**

- ***The Play:*** *Set up a* ***Google Alert*** *for news related to your niche (e.g., "data breach," "FTC investigation"). When a major story breaks, feed the article into* ***Claude*** *and prompt it:* "From the perspective of a data privacy lawyer, what are the top 3 immediate legal risks for other companies mentioned in this article? Draft a short, authoritative LinkedIn post about it."
- ***Your Human Touch:*** *Review the post for accuracy and add a crucial sentence:* "This is a developing situation, and this is not legal advice. But it's a critical reminder for all companies to review their own data handling policies." *This provides timely, valuable insight while maintaining ethical boundaries.*

**The "De-Risking" Comment Strategy:**

- ***The Play:*** *Follow tech founders, VCs, and CEOs in the industries you serve. When they post about a new product launch or a significant company initiative, use* ***ChatGPT*** *to help* *you plan a thoughtful, value-adding comment. Prompt:* "A CEO just posted about their new AI-driven product. What is a potential legal or ethical consideration they might not be thinking about? Frame it as a supportive, insightful question."

***Your Human Touch:*** *Post the question. Example:* "This looks like a game-changer! A fascinating question from a legal perspective is how to navigate the data privacy implications of user-generated data. It's a challenge for the whole industry." *This shows your expertise in a helpful, non-promotional way, making you a trusted voice in their network.*

## Final Thoughts: AI Won't Argue in Court (But It Will Give You an Edge Over Lawyers Who Don't Use It)

AI won't replace lawyers. But it *will* replace lawyers who refuse to adapt to the new era of legal tech.

The best attorneys aren't using AI because they *have* to—they're using it because it makes them more efficient, more informed, and ultimately, more successful.

So stop wasting time on manual contract review, endless legal research, and mind-numbing document analysis. Let

AI handle the tedious tasks—so you can focus on strategy, advocacy, and winning cases.

Your billable hours (and your sanity) will thank you.

# AI FOR HEALTHCARE

## SMARTER DIAGNOSES, FEWER PAPERWORK HEADACHES, AND MAYBE EVEN A LUNCH BREAK

### *Why AI Won't Replace Doctors, But It Will Keep Them From Losing Their Minds*

IF YOU WORK IN HEALTHCARE, YOU'RE OVERWORKED. I DON'T even need to ask. Whether you're a doctor, nurse, administrator, or researcher, the industry runs on high stakes, long hours, and mountains of documentation.

Now, imagine a world where AI could sift through medical records in seconds, generate accurate patient notes automatically, and even help diagnose illnesses with better precision than a sleep-deprived resident on their third overnight shift.

That world is already here. AI is transforming healthcare, making it faster, more efficient, and—dare we say—less exhausting.

And no, this doesn't mean robots replacing doctors (at least, not yet). It means AI handles tedious, time-consuming tasks, so healthcare professionals can focus on patients, not paperwork.

So if you're tired of drowning in admin work, chasing down lab results, or manually documenting every single patient encounter, it's time to let AI help you breathe again.

### The AI Revolution in Healthcare: What's Changing?

AI in healthcare isn't about taking over—it's about taking the load off.

From faster diagnoses to predictive analytics to automated documentation, AI is enabling healthcare providers to **work smarter, not harder.**

What AI is Doing for Healthcare Right Now:

- **AI-Assisted Diagnoses**—AI-powered imaging tools are detecting cancers, fractures, and anomalies with incredible accuracy.
- **Automating Administrative Work**—AI transcribes patient visits, summarizes notes, and streamlines data entry, reducing paperwork nightmares.
- **Predicting Patient Outcomes**—AI analyzes patient history and real-time vitals to anticipate risks before they become emergencies.
- **Improving Personalized Medicine**—AI can tailor

treatments to individual patients based on genetic and lifestyle data.

- **Enhancing Drug Discovery & Research**—
  AI analyzes massive datasets to identify new drug candidates faster than human researchers ever could.

And the best part? AI doesn't need sleep, coffee, or overtime pay.

### The Best AI Tools for Healthcare Professionals

AI is already making waves in hospitals, clinics, and research labs. Below are some of the top AI-powered tools that are changing the game. You are still responsible for choosing the right tools for your purposes and checking on the latest updates as the tool choices are changing fast.

#### AI for Diagnosing & Medical Imaging

**Viz.ai**—AI-powered stroke detection tool that instantly analyzes CT scans and alerts doctors in real time.

> ***Best Use:*** *Faster stroke intervention (because minutes matter).*
> ***Watch Out For:*** *Works alongside radiologists, not as a replacement.*

**PathAI**—AI that analyzes pathology slides to detect cancers and abnormalities with high precision.

> ***Best Use:*** *Enhancing pathologists' diagnostic accuracy.*
> ***Watch Out For:*** *AI still requires human validation.*

**Qure.ai**—AI-driven radiology tool that scans X-rays and CT scans for signs of pneumonia, fractures, and TB.

> ***Best Use:*** *Triage & prioritization in radiology departments.*
> ***Watch Out For:*** *False positives; therefore, human review is still essential.*

**AI for Clinical Documentation & Workflow Automation**

**Nuance DAX (Dragon Ambient eXperience)**—AI-powered speech recognition that listens to doctor-patient interactions and auto-generates clinical notes.

> ***Best Use:*** *Reducing physician burnout from documentation overload.*
> ***Watch Out For:*** *Still requires final review and approval.*

**Suki AI**—A digital AI-powered medical assistant that writes patient notes, orders prescriptions, and even retrieves patient history on command.

***Best Use:*** *Doctors looking to reclaim hours lost to paperwork.*
***Watch Out For:*** *Works best when trained on specific medical workflows.*

**HealthTensor**—AI that reviews patient records and suggests diagnoses based on past data—essentially an extra set of eyes on patient history.

***Best Use:*** *Detecting overlooked conditions.*
***Watch Out For:*** *AI is excellent at surfacing information, but humans make the call.*

**AI for Predictive Analytics & Risk Assessment**

**Tempus**—AI-powered genomic sequencing & predictive analytics tool for personalized cancer treatment.

***Best Use:*** *Precision medicine & tailored treatments.*
***Watch Out For:*** *Costly for smaller clinics.*

**Epic's AI-Powered Sepsis Model**—AI-driven early sepsis detection that analyzes vitals and lab results in real time.

***Best Use:*** *Preventing life-threatening sepsis before it escalates.*
***Watch Out For:*** *Best used as a warning system, not a sole diagnostic tool.*

**Medopad AI**—an AI-powered remote patient monitoring system that tracks chronic conditions using wearable data.

> ***Best Use:*** *Telemedicine & chronic disease management.*
> ***Watch Out For:*** *AI-generated alerts need physician oversight.*

**AI for Drug Discovery & Research**

**AlphaFold (by DeepMind)**—AI that predicts protein structures in minutes—a breakthrough for drug development & genetic research.

> ***Best Use:*** *Speeding up pharmaceutical research.*
> ***Watch Out For:*** *Not every structure prediction leads to a viable drug.*

**BenevolentAI**—an AI-powered drug discovery platform that analyzes massive datasets to identify potential new treatments.

> ***Best Use:*** *Pharmaceutical R&D & clinical trials.*
> ***Watch Out For:*** *AI helps identify candidates, but clinical validation still takes time.*

## Step-by-Step: Using AI to Reduce Workload in Healthcare

Let's walk through a real-world AI-powered workflow—from diagnosis to documentation.

💡 **Scenario:** You're a physician seeing 15+ patients a day. Here's how AI can streamline your workflow and reduce stress.

### Step 1: AI-Assisted Diagnosis & Imaging

- A patient arrives with chest pain.
- You order an X-ray, and **Qure.ai** immediately flags an anomaly before the radiologist even reviews it.
- You receive AI-assisted insights that help you decide whether to order more tests.

### Step 2: AI-Generated Clinical Documentation

- Instead of typing notes, **Nuance DAX** records the visit in real time.
- AI generates a structured clinical note—you review & approve before filing.

### Step 3: Predictive Risk Analysis

- The patient has mild symptoms, but **Epic's AI sepsis model** suggests a high-risk flag based on lab results.

- You decide to admit & monitor the patient before symptoms worsen.

**Step 4: Automated Follow-Up & Patient Monitoring**

- The patient is discharged, and **Medopad AI** continues to monitor their vitals remotely.
- AI alerts you if there's a decline so that you can intervene sooner.

**LinkedIn Personal Branding for the Healthcare Innovator**

For healthcare professionals, a LinkedIn brand is about showcasing a commitment to patient outcomes, innovation, and the future of medicine. It's a platform to share knowledge with peers, advocate for new technologies, and establish yourself as a leader in the shift towards value-based, tech-enabled care.

**Your Goal:** To be known as a healthcare professional who is not only an expert clinician or administrator but also a leader in shaping the future of the industry.

**AI-Powered Plays for Your LinkedIn Brand:**

**The "Clinical Research Digest" Post:**

***The Play:*** *Use* ***Elicit*** *or* ***Consensus**** *to find and summarize three new peer-reviewed studies related to your specialty (e.g., "AI in diagnostic imaging," "telemedicine adoption rates"). Ask the AI:* "Summarize the key findings from these three studies on AI in radiology. What is the common thread, and what is the most significant implication for clinical practice?"

***Your Human Touch:*** *Post the digest with your own expert opinion.* "Fascinating to see the growing consensus on AI's role in improving diagnostic accuracy. While the tech is impressive, the real challenge remains: how do we integrate these tools into clinical workflows without increasing physician burnout? Here's my take..." *This elevates you from a practitioner to a thought leader on implementation.*

**The "Patient Experience" Story:**

***The Play:*** *Reflect on a recent (and fully anonymized) patient interaction where*

---

* Elicit focuses on automating and enhancing the literature review process, helping researchers understand complex topics and synthesize information. Consensus, on the other hand, is designed as an AI search engine that finds relevant insights from research papers and synthesizes them, providing quick answers to research questions.

*technology played a key role.*
*Use* **ChatGPT** *to help you structure the story. Prompt:* "Write a short, compelling story about how a new digital check-in system reduced a patient's anxiety and wait time. Focus on the human impact, not the technology. Follow a 'Challenge-Solution-Outcome' narrative."

***Your Human Touch:*** *Share the story. This humanizes your work and demonstrates that a desire for better patient outcomes drives your focus on technology. It's a powerful way to build a brand that is both empathetic and respected.*

**The "Cross-Disciplinary" Commenting Strategy:**

***The Play:*** *Your expertise is valuable outside of healthcare circles. Follow leaders in health-tech, venture capital, and public policy. When they post about the business or technology of healthcare, use an AI tool to help you translate your clinical experience into their language. Prompt* ***Claude:*** "A VC just posted about investing in a new AI scribe tool. As a physician who has used these tools, what are two key due diligence questions they should ask about clinical workflow integration and data security? Draft a respectful, insightful comment."

***Your Human Touch:*** *Post the comment. This bridges the gap between the clinical and business worlds, positioning you as a rare and valuable expert who understands both.*

## Final Thoughts: AI Won't Replace Doctors—But It Will Help Them Stay Sane

Healthcare isn't getting any easier, but AI can make it more manageable.

Instead of spending hours buried in documentation, chasing lab results, or sifting through thousands of patient records, let AI handle the administrative burden so you can focus on patient care.

Doctors, nurses, and healthcare professionals will always be essential—but those who use AI effectively will be freed up to spend more time listening to patients and improving both their experience and outcomes.

So the choice is simple: keep drowning in paperwork, or start using AI to make your job (and your life) a whole lot easier.

Your patients (and your sanity) will thank you.

# AI FOR EDUCATION

## FROM OVERWORKED TO OVERACHIEVING (WITHOUT LOSING YOUR MIND)

***How AI is Helping Educators Teach Smarter, Grade Faster, and Finally Take a Breath***

TEACHERS AND EDUCATORS: YOU'RE SUPERHEROES, BUT LET'S be honest—you're exhausted superheroes. Between lesson planning, grading, keeping students engaged, and trying to prevent AI-powered cheating, your workload has reached Olympic levels.

The good news? AI isn't here to replace you—it's here to help you.

Imagine having an AI-powered assistant that could generate lesson plans, grade assignments, personalize learning for each student, and even detect plagiarism before your students think they've outsmarted you. That's not the future—it's happening right now.

So whether you're a K-12 teacher, college professor, or online educator, this chapter will show you how to work smarter, not harder—while making sure your students are actually learning (and not just copy-pasting from ChatGPT).

### AI's Role in Modern Education – What's Changing?

AI is not here to replace teachers. Let's say that again for the people in the back.

It's here to help with the tedious stuff, so educators can spend more time teaching instead of getting lost in administrative chaos.

What AI is Doing for Educators Right Now:

- **Automating Lesson Planning**—AI can

generate entire lesson plans, worksheets, quizzes, and even interactive activities in minutes.

- **Personalizing Learning**—AI-driven tutoring tools adjust content based on student progress and learning styles—because not all students learn at the same pace.
- **Grading Assignments Faster**—AI-powered grading tools can evaluate multiple-choice, short-answer, and even essay-style questions in record time.
- **Preventing AI-Generated Plagiarism**—AI detection tools can identify AI-written essays and assignments, ensuring students cannot simply copy and paste their way through school.
- **Enhancing Student Engagement**—AI-powered chatbots and virtual tutors answer student questions 24/7, even when teachers are off the clock.
- **Predict at-risk students** before they begin to fall behind.

**The best part?** AI is doing all this while reducing teacher burnout and freeing up time for what matters—actual teaching.

### The Best AI Tools for Educators

Let's get straight to it: Which AI tools should educators be using? Here's a breakdown of the most effective AI-powered platforms for lesson planning, grading, and student engagement.

### AI for Lesson Planning & Content Creation

**MagicSchool AI**—AI-powered lesson planner that generates quizzes, rubrics, scaffolding activities, and differentiated instruction plans based on any subject or grade level.

> ***Best Use:*** *Teachers who want high-quality, pre-built resources in minutes.*
> ***Watch Out For:*** *AI-generated lessons* ***still need human review*** *for accuracy.*

**ChatGPT (OpenAI)**—Great for brainstorming lesson ideas, simplifying complex topics, and generating student-friendly explanations.

> ***Best Use:*** *Creating lesson outlines, writing prompts, or summarizing complex concepts.*
> ***Watch Out For:*** *AI sometimes hallucinates information—always fact-check.*

**Nolej AI** – Transforms existing documents, articles, or videos into interactive learning modules with built-in quizzes.

> ***Best Use:*** *Turning passive content into interactive learning experiences.*
> ***Watch Out For:*** *Works best with well-structured educational materials.*

**AI for Grading & Feedback**

**Gradescope AI**—Automates the grading of multiple-choice, short-answer, and even long-form essays with AI-powered pattern recognition.

> ***Best Use:*** *Teachers who want to cut grading time in half.*
> ***Watch Out For:*** *AI can misinterpret creative answers—manual review is still needed.*

**Turnitin's AI Detection Tool**—Identifies whether students have used AI to generate essays or assignments(because, yes, they're trying).

> ***Best Use:*** *Academic integrity enforcement.*
> ***Watch Out For:*** *False positives , so always review flagged content before taking action.*

**Scribo AI**—an AI-powered writing feedback tool that helps students improve their essays by offering AI-generated writing suggestions.

***Best Use:*** *Helping students refine their writing before final submission.*
***Watch Out For:*** *Students still need to learn proper writing skills—AI shouldn't do all the work.*

**AI for Student Engagement & Tutoring**

**Khanmigo (by Khan Academy)**—An AI tutor that helps students with math, reading comprehension, and interactive discussions tailored to their learning level.

***Best Use:*** *Supplemental AI tutoring for students who need extra help.*
***Watch Out For:*** *Not a replacement for real human guidance.*

**Quizlet AI**—Generates AI-powered flashcards, quizzes, and practice tests for self-paced learning.

***Best Use:*** *Helping students reinforce knowledge through active recall.*
***Watch Out For:*** *AI-generated questions; they can sometimes oversimplify concepts.*

**Socratic (by Google)**—AI-powered educational search tool that helps students get instant answers with explanations for homework questions.

***Best Use:*** *Providing just-in-time help when students are stuck on specific homework problems.*

***Watch Out For:*** *Students might rely on quick answers rather than developing problem-solving skills.*

### Step-by-Step: Using AI to Save Time & Improve Learning

Let's go through a real-world AI-powered education workflow—from lesson planning to grading.

#### Scenario 1: AI-powered education workflow

You're a high school teacher planning a unit on climate change. Here's how AI can streamline your work while keeping students engaged.

1. **Generate a Complete Lesson Plan**
    - Use **MagicSchool AI** to create a complete lesson outline, including objectives, activities, and assessments.
    - Review and refine AI-generated content to align with your teaching style.
2. **Create AI-Powered Learning Materials**
    - Use **Nolej AI** to turn an article on climate change into an interactive lesson with embedded questions.

   - Use **Quizlet AI** to generate flashcards and quizzes based on key concepts.
3. **Use AI-Generated Writing Feedback**
   - Assign an essay on "**The Impact of Climate Change on Local Communities.**"
   - Have students run drafts through Scribo AI to get AI-powered writing feedback before submission.
4. **Automate Grading & AI Detection**
   - Use **Gradescope AI** to grade short answers and essays faster.
   - Run assignments through **Turnitin's AI detector** to check for AI-generated writing.
5. **Enhance Engagement with AI Tutoring**
   - Direct struggling students to **Khanmigo** for AI-powered tutoring sessions.
   - Encourage students to use **Socratic AI** for research questions instead of Google.

## Scenario 2: AI-Powered Student Learning & Support

1. **Personalizing Student Learning**
   - Implement **Squirrel AI** to provide adaptive learning paths based on individual student performance.
   - AI identifies weak areas and adjusts lessons, offering additional practice exercises.
2. **Automating Grading & Feedback**

- Use **Gradescope AI** to speed up assignment grading and provide instant feedback.
- AI-generated feedback helps students identify and correct mistakes, improving their learning outcomes.

3. **Enhancing Student Engagement**
    - Deploy **Khanmigo** to offer AI-driven tutoring and real-time academic support.
    - AI-powered chatbots assist in answering student queries and provide access to learning resources.
4. **Optimizing Administrative Processes**
    - Use **Salesforce for Education** to track student engagement and improve recruitment strategies.
    - AI-driven predictive analytics help institutions identify students at risk of dropping out and intervene accordingly.

## The Future of AI in Education—What's Next?

AI isn't going away—it's evolving rapidly, and educators who embrace it will be better prepared for the future of learning.

What's Coming Next?

**AI-Powered Adaptive Learning**—Fully personalized AI tutors that adjust in real-time to a student's knowledge gaps.

**AI-Powered Lesson Simulations**—Virtual reality and AI-generated interactive lessons where students learn through real-world scenarios.

**AI-Driven Teacher Assistants**—AI chatbots that handle routine admin tasks, parent communication, and lesson prep.

## Final Thoughts: AI Won't Replace Teachers—But Teachers Who Use AI Will Have an Edge

Teachers aren't going anywhere—but the ones who learn to use AI effectively will have more time, better tools, and less stress.

So if you're still spending hours grading, rewriting lesson plans, or battling AI-powered student plagiarism, it's time to flip the script.

Start using AI to lighten your workload, improve student engagement, and bring education into the future.

Because the best teachers don't just adapt to change—they lead it.

# AI FOR SMALL BUSINESS OWNERS AND ENTREPRENEURS

*How to Run Your Business Like a Fortune 500 CEO (Without the Staff, Budget, or Nervous Breakdown)*

IF YOU'RE A SMALL BUSINESS OWNER, SOLOPRENEUR, OR freelancer, you wear all the hats—marketer, sales rep, customer service agent, accountant, and occasional IT specialist when your website crashes at the worst possible moment.

AI won't run your business for you (yet), but it can automate, optimize, and streamline so many tasks that you'll feel like you suddenly have an extra pair of hands—and maybe even a few extra hours in your day.

From writing social media posts to handling customer inquiries, from managing finances to predicting sales trends, AI is the secret weapon small businesses need to stay competitive without burning out.

So if you're tired of doing everything manually, let's talk about how AI can do the heavy lifting—while you focus on growing your business (or at least taking a coffee break without feeling guilty).

## Why Small Businesses Need AI (Like, Right Now)

Large corporations have teams for everything. You have... yourself, a laptop, and a caffeine habit.

### What AI is Doing for Small Business Owners Right Now:

- **Automating Marketing & Social Media** – AI can write blog posts, social media captions, and ad copy while you focus on your actual business.
- **Handling Customer Support 24/7** – AI-powered

chatbots can answer FAQs, book appointments, and respond to inquiries even while you sleep.

- **Optimizing Sales & Lead Generation** – AI analyzes customer behavior and sales data to predict which leads are most likely to convert.
- **Automating Accounting & Finances** – AI-powered bookkeeping tools categorize expenses, generate reports, and even forecast cash flow trends.
- **Boosting Productivity & Time Management** – AI can schedule meetings, draft emails, and automate repetitive tasks so you can focus on the big picture.

**The Bottom Line:**

AI won't replace your business instincts. But it *will* take care of the boring, repetitive, and time-consuming stuff so you can focus on what matters—growth, customers, and making more money.

### The AI Tools Every Small Business Owner Needs

There's no shortage of AI tools, but you don't need all of them. Here are the most practical and effective AI solutions for small businesses and entrepreneurs.

#### AI for Marketing & Content Creation

**ChatGPT / Jasper AI**—AI-powered copywriting tools that

generate blogs, social media posts, product descriptions, and ad copy in seconds.

> ***Best Use:* Content creation on demand** *when you don't have time to write everything yourself.*
> ***Watch Out For:* AI can sound generic***—always tweak to match your brand voice.*

**Canva AI**—AI-powered graphic design for logos, social media posts, flyers, and ads—no design skills required.

> ***Best Use:*** *Quickly creating professional-looking visuals for marketing.*
> ***Watch Out For:*** *AI-generated images may need manual tweaks for branding consistency.*

**Lumen5**—AI video creator that turns blog posts into short, engaging videos for social media.

> ***Best Use:*** *Creating marketing videos without hiring a videographer.*
> ***Watch Out For:*** *AI won't match high-end video production quality - yet!*

I say "yet" because, in the last year. At the same time, producing employee training videos for a client, the quality difference from when I started to now of AI-generated avatars, generative video, and AI production tools in general is night and day.

## AI for Customer Service & Chatbots

**ManyChat**—an AI-powered chatbot for Facebook Messenger, WhatsApp, and Instagram, automating customer responses and lead generation.

> ***Best Use:*** *Answering FAQs and capturing leads on social media.*
> ***Watch Out For:*** *AI chatbots can't handle complex issues—have a human fallback.*

**Intercom AI**—AI-driven customer support that answers inquiries, books appointments, and resolves common issues.

> ***Best Use:*** *Handling customer service without hiring a full-time rep.*
> ***Watch Out For:*** *AI-generated responses need periodic updates.*

**Tidio**—AI-powered live chat for websites that provides instant customer support and even suggests responses.

> ***Best Use:*** *Engaging website visitors and converting them into customers.*

***Watch Out For:*** *AI chatbots need training to provide accurate answers.*

## AI for Sales & Lead Generation

**HubSpot Sales Hub AI**—AI-powered CRM that scores leads, suggests email responses, and automates follow-ups.

***Best Use:*** *Managing sales leads without spending all day in your inbox.*
***Watch Out For:*** *It's powerful, but best suited for businesses that get a lot of inbound leads.*

**Seventh Sense AI**—an AI email marketing tool that optimizes send times and personalization based on customer behavior.

***Best Use:*** *Boosting email open rates and engagement.*
***Watch Out For:*** *Works best with an active email list—won't perform miracles if your list is dead.*

**Crystal Knows**—an AI-powered personality analysis tool that helps you tailor sales pitches based on customer personality types.

> ***Best Use:*** *Writing personalized outreach emails that convert.*
> ***Watch Out For:*** *AI-generated insights aren't foolproof—use them as a guide, not gospel.*

## AI for Finance & Bookkeeping

**QuickBooks AI**—AI-powered bookkeeping that categorizes expenses, generates reports, and predicts cash flow.

> ***Best Use:*** *Small business owners who want automated financial tracking.*
> ***Watch Out For:*** *AI can miscategorize transactions—double-check reports.*

**Fathom AI**—AI-powered financial analytics that provide cash flow forecasting and business performance insights.

> ***Best Use:*** *Planning for future growth and avoiding cash crunches.*
> ***Watch Out For:*** *AI predictions depend on accurate financial data.*

**Xero AI**—AI-assisted accounting software that reconciles transactions and automates invoices.

***Best Use:*** *Managing finances without hiring an accountant.*
***Watch Out For:*** *Needs proper setup to categorize expenses correctly.*

## Step-by-Step: Using AI to Automate Your Business

Let's say you're a solopreneur running an online business. Here's how you can utilize AI to save time, boost sales, and alleviate headaches.

### Step 1: Automate Marketing & Content Creation

- Use **ChatGPT** to generate blog post topics, product descriptions, and social media captions.
- Use **Canva AI** to create ad graphics and marketing visuals.
- Use **Lumen5** to turn blog posts into short promotional videos.

### Step 2: Set Up AI-Powered Customer Service

- Use **ManyChat** to automate customer interactions on Facebook & Instagram.
- Use **Tidio AI Chatbot** to answer questions on your website 24/7.
- Use **Intercom AI** to automate appointment scheduling & support tickets.

**Step 3: Automate Sales & Lead Generation**

- Use **HubSpot Sales Hub AI** to score leads and automate follow-ups.
- Use **Seventh Sense AI** to send marketing emails at the perfect time.
- Use **Crystal Knows** to personalize sales outreach messages.

**Step 4: Streamline Finance & Accounting**

- Use **QuickBooks AI** to track expenses and categorize transactions.
- Use **Fathom AI** to predict cash flow and optimize spending.
- Use **Xero AI** to automate invoicing & payment reminders.

## LinkedIn Personal Branding for the Scrappy Entrepreneur

For small business owners, you *are* the brand. Your personal LinkedIn profile is often more potent than your company page. It's where you share your vision, your struggles, and your expertise. A strong personal brand builds a community around your business and attracts talent, partners, and customers who believe in your mission.

**Your Goal:** To build a loyal community that is invested in your journey and eager to support your business.

**AI-Powered Plays for Your LinkedIn Brand:**

**The "Build in Public" Update:**

- ***The Play:*** *At the end of each week, dictate your thoughts into* **Otter.ai**. *Talk about one win, one challenge, and one thing you learned. Feed the transcript to* **ChatGPT** *and prompt it:* "Turn this weekly reflection into a short, authentic 'behind-the-scenes' LinkedIn post. Be vulnerable about the challenge but optimistic about the solution. End with a question to the community."
- ***Your Human Touch:*** *Share the post. This transparency is magnetic. It makes your audience feel like insiders and builds a powerful, authentic connection that corporate-speak never can. Example:* "This week was a rollercoaster! We finally landed [Win], but struggled with [Challenge]. The big lesson was [Learning]. For other founders, how do you stay motivated when things get tough?"

**The "Content Repurposing" Engine:**

***The Play:*** *You wrote one blog post or recorded one podcast. Use* **Claude** *to turn it into a week's worth of LinkedIn content. Prompt:* "Analyze this blog post. Extract five key quotes, three surprising statistics, and two actionable tips. Write a unique LinkedIn post for each of these 10 items."

***Your Human Touch:*** *Schedule these posts using a simple tool like Buffer or Hootsuite. This allows you to create a massive amount of value from a single piece of content, ensuring you stay top-of-mind with your audience without burning out.*

**The "Tool and Resource" Carousel:**

***The Play:*** *Think about the non-competitive tools and resources that help you run your business. Use* **ChatGPT** *to create a carousel post. Prompt:* "Create a 5-slide LinkedIn carousel on 'The 5 Tools I Can't Live Without as a Small Business Owner.' For each tool, briefly explain the problem it solves."

***Your Human Touch:*** *Design it in* ***Canva*** *and share it. This is pure value for your audience of fellow entrepreneurs. You are helping them solve their problems, which builds immense trust and positions you as a helpful hub of information in your network.*

## Final Thoughts: AI Won't Replace Entrepreneurs, But Entrepreneurs Who Use AI Will Win

AI isn't here to run your business for you—but it *is* here to make your life significantly easier.

So if you're still manually writing marketing copy, tracking sales leads by hand, or spending hours on bookkeeping, it's time to let AI do the heavy lifting.

The future belongs to business owners who leverage AI to work smarter, scale faster, and stay ahead.

The question is: Will you be one of them?

# AI FOR HUMAN RESOURCES & RECRUITING

*How AI is Revolutionizing Talent Acquisition, Employee Engagement, and Workforce Management*

## The AI-Powered HR Revolution: More Bots, Less Burnout

Human Resources used to be all about endless paperwork, frantic hiring, and trying to decode cryptic employee complaints (like why the coffee machine only works when you kick it twice). But now, AI is swooping in to automate the grunt work, streamline hiring, and—most importantly—help HR pros focus on actual people instead of endless spreadsheets.

AI-powered automation is revolutionizing traditional HR tasks. Resume screening? AI can scan thousands of applications before you finish your morning coffee. Candidate assessments? AI identifies top talent with predictive analytics that work—unlike that gut feeling that led to hiring "Steve from Sales" who turned out to be a walking disaster. Employee engagement? AI analyzes workforce trends to help keep employees happy, engaged, and less likely to ghost you for another job.

Companies that embrace AI in HR aren't just surviving, they're thriving. From AI-driven chatbots handling HR inquiries faster than an over-caffeinated intern to predictive analytics forecasting who's about to quit, AI is shaping the future of HR by making workplaces more innovative, more efficient, and—dare we say—more human.

## Why AI is the Best HR Assistant You'll Never Have to Fire

The job of HR has evolved beyond simply hiring and firing. AI is now transforming everything from talent acquisition to workforce planning, employee engagement, and performance management. Using AI, HR professionals recruit faster, improve employee retention, and handle mundane tasks more efficiently.

AI helps HR teams:

- **Hire smarter:** AI finds the best candidates by analyzing skills, experience, and even personality traits. (So no more hiring based on "I liked their handshake.")
- **Keep employees happy:** AI monitors engagement and flags potential burnout before it escalates into rage-quitting via email.
- **Automate the soul-sucking tasks:** Let AI handle paperwork, scheduling, and compliance tracking while HR professionals focus on strategy and culture.

With AI, HR isn't just surviving—it's thriving. Who should be the only ones who are nervous? That pile of old paper resumes gathering dust in the back office.

. . .

## Current AI Adoption Trends in HR

- Over 65% of recruiters use AI-driven applicant tracking systems (ATS) to automate resume screening and candidate ranking.
- AI-based pre-hire assessments increase job-matching accuracy by 40%.
- AI-powered chatbots handle over 50% of routine HR inquiries, reducing administrative workload.
- By leveraging AI, HR professionals can improve efficiency, enhance decision-making, and create more personalized employee experiences.

## Key AI Tools for HR & Recruiting

A breakdown of AI tools for different HR functions, including their pros, cons, and best use cases.

### AI-Powered Talent Acquisition & Recruiting

AI can enhance candidate sourcing and job matching, making hiring faster and more accurate.

> ***Best for:*** *Large-scale hiring, reducing recruiter workload, and better job-candidate matching.*
>
> ***Limitations:*** *Some tools require large datasets to work effectively.*

**HireEZ (formerly Hiretual):** AI-driven talent sourcing that scans LinkedIn, job boards, and databases to find the best-fit candidates.

> ***Best Use:*** *Finding passive candidates for hard-to-fill technical or specialized roles.*
> ***Watch Out For:*** *Over-reliance on digital footprints may miss qualified candidates with limited online presence.*

**Eightfold AI:** Uses predictive analytics to match job seekers with the right roles based on skills and experience.

> ***Best Use:*** *Career pathing and internal mobility to keep top talent.*
> ***Watch Out For:*** *Needs substantial historical hiring data to make accurate predictions.*

**Pymetrics:** AI-driven soft skills assessments using neuroscience-based games to evaluate candidates.

> ***Best Use:*** *Reducing unconscious bias in early screening stages.*
> ***Watch Out For:*** *Games might create a disconnected candidate experience if not adequately explained.*

## AI-Enhanced Resume Screening & ATS (Applicant Tracking Systems)

AI automates candidate screening and reduces unconscious bias in hiring.

> ***Best for:*** *Automating resume screening, ranking top candidates.*
> ***Limitations:*** *AI algorithms must be closely monitored to prevent reinforcing existing biases.*

**Greenhouse ATS & Lever:** AI-powered resume ranking based on job fit, reducing manual screening time.

> ***Best Use:*** *High-volume recruiting where hundreds of applications need quick processing.*
> ***Watch Out For:*** *Algorithms may inadvertently screen out non-traditional career paths.*

**LinkedIn Talent Insights:** Uses AI to identify top candidates and benchmark hiring trends.

> ***Best Use:*** *Market intelligence for competitive talent pools and compensation benchmarking.*

> ***Watch Out For:*** *Data is limited to LinkedIn users and may not accurately represent all industries.*

**Manatal:** AI resume screening with social media profile enrichment.

> ***Best Use:*** *Creating comprehensive candidate profiles beyond the resume.*
> ***Watch Out For:*** *Privacy concerns when pulling social media data—ensure compliance with local laws.*

### AI-Driven Employee Engagement & Performance Management

AI helps improve retention, predict employee satisfaction, and tailor HR strategies to individual needs.

> ***Best for:*** *Preventing employee turnover, improving company culture.*
> ***Limitations:*** *Requires HR teams to interpret AI insights and act accordingly.*

**Lattice AI & Culture Amp:** AI-powered performance tracking and engagement surveys.

***Best Use:*** *Identifying engagement trends and predicting retention issues before they escalate.*

***Watch Out For:*** *Survey fatigue—even AI-powered tools shouldn't overwhelm employees with constant feedback requests.*

**Workday AI:** Uses predictive analytics to identify employee flight risk and training needs.

***Best Use:*** *Proactive retention strategies for high-performing employees.*

***Watch Out For:*** *False positives that may lead managers to worry unnecessarily about valued employees leaving.*

**Humu:** AI-based behavioral nudges to enhance leadership effectiveness and employee satisfaction.

***Best Use:*** *Delivering personalized micro-coaching to managers and employees.*

***Watch Out For:*** *Nudges can feel intrusive if not implemented with transparency.*

**AI Chatbots & Virtual HR Assistants**

AI chatbots streamline HR workflows and improve employee experience.

> ***Best for:*** *Reducing repetitive HR tasks, handling employee inquiries.*
> ***Limitations:*** *Chatbots are capable of handling simple queries but may struggle with more complex HR cases.*

**Paradox Olivia:** AI chatbot for candidate screening and interview scheduling.

> ***Best Use:*** *Handling high-volume initial candidate conversations and scheduling.*
> ***Watch Out For:*** *May struggle with nuanced questions about company culture from candidates.*

**Leena AI:** Automates employee FAQs, PTO requests, and HR policy inquiries.

> ***Best Use:*** *24/7 HR support for global teams across time zones.*
> ***Watch Out For:*** *Requires regular updates to ensure policies are current and avoid providing outdated information.*

**ChatGPT for HR:** Customizable AI for internal employee support.

> ***Best Use:*** *Creating custom HR content, policy summaries, and onboarding materials.*
>
> ***Watch Out For:*** *Requires proper guardrails to prevent the sharing of confidential HR information.*

## AI for Workforce Planning & HR Analytics

AI tools help HR leaders make data-driven workforce decisions.

> ***Best for:*** *Workforce analytics, strategic planning.*
>
> ***Limitations:*** *Requires HR teams to be data-savvy for best results.*

**Visier:** Predicts workforce needs, retention risks, and hiring trends.

> ***Best Use:*** *Strategic workforce planning and succession management.*
>
> ***Watch Out For:*** *Requires clean, consistent HR data for accurate predictions.*

**SAP SuccessFactors:** AI-powered HR analytics to forecast skills gaps.

> ***Best Use:*** *Long-term skills development planning and learning program design.*
> ***Watch Out For:*** *Complex implementation that requires specialized expertise.*

**Oracle HCM Cloud:** AI-driven workforce management and payroll optimization.

> ***Best Use:*** *Integrated HR operations from recruitment through retirement.*
> ***Watch Out For:*** *Significant investment in implementation and change management.*

### AI Best Practices for HR Professionals

- Use AI to assist, not replace, human judgment.
- Monitor AI hiring bias and algorithm fairness.
- Ensure AI tools comply with HR privacy regulations (GDPR, EEOC, etc.).
- Train HR teams to work in tandem with AI for improved decision-making.

### The Future of AI in HR

AI is continuously evolving in the HR space, with future trends including:

- AI-driven workforce planning.
- Personalized AI training and learning platforms.
- Ethical AI frameworks for unbiased hiring.

**Next Steps for HR Professionals**

- Choose one AI tool to test in your HR workflow this month.
- Evaluate AI's impact on hiring efficiency and employee engagement.
- Stay updated on AI ethics and compliance regulations.

**LinkedIn Personal Branding for the Strategic HR Leader**

The best HR and recruiting professionals are no longer seen as administrative gatekeepers. They are strategic partners who shape company culture, attract top talent, and drive business outcomes. Your LinkedIn brand should reflect this shift. It's your platform to showcase your expertise in the future of work, talent strategy, and building successful teams.

**Your Goal:** To attract A-level talent to your company and be seen as a thought leader by your peers in the HR community.

. . .

**AI-Powered Plays for Your LinkedIn Brand:**

**The "Talent Market" Data Post:**

***The Play:*** *Use* ***Perplexity AI*** *to find recent reports or articles on talent trends in your industry (e.g., "remote work satisfaction," "skills-based hiring statistics," "employee retention drivers"). Ask the AI:* "Summarize the top 3 most surprising statistics from this report on the current state of the tech talent market."

***Your Human Touch:*** *Share these statistics in a LinkedIn post, but add your analysis.* "The data is in: 65% of developers now prioritize flexible work over a higher salary. For companies still mandating a 5-day office week, this isn't a preference—it's a competitive disadvantage. Here's how we're adapting our talent strategy..." *This shows you are a data-driven, strategic HR leader, not just a recruiter.*

**The "Candidate Experience" Teardown:**

***The Play:*** *Anonymously document a positive or negative candidate experience you've* *observed. Use* **ChatGPT** *to structure it as a lesson. Prompt:* "Write a short LinkedIn post about the importance of candidate experience. Tell a story about how a simple, personalized rejection letter can create a brand advocate, while a 'ghosting' experience can create a brand detractor. Frame it as a lesson for other hiring managers."

***Your Human Touch:*** *Post this story. It shows your empathy and your commitment to treating people with respect, which is highly attractive to potential candidates. It shows you are building a culture of excellence, not just filling seats.*

**The "Company Culture" Showcase:**

***The Play:*** *Use an AI image generator like* **Midjourney** *with a creative prompt to create a unique, eye-catching image that represents your company culture (e.g., "a team of diverse people collaborating to build a bridge of light, cinematic style").*

***Your Human Touch:*** *Pair this unique image with a post written by you (or assisted by* **Claude***) that tells a real story about your* *company culture in action. The distinctive visual will stop the scroll, and the authentic story will make the message stick. This is far more effective than another generic team photo.*

# AI FOR FINANCE & ACCOUNTING

*How AI is Transforming Financial Management, Risk Analysis, and Business Strategy*

## AI: The Accountant That Never Takes a Coffee Break (or Loses a Receipt)

The financial industry is getting a serious upgrade, and it's not just another Excel plugin. AI is stepping in to automate bookkeeping, catch fraudsters, predict economic trends, and make CFOs look like geniuses. From reconciling transactions to detecting anomalies, AI is revolutionizing finance by eliminating human errors and uncovering insights that even the best number crunchers might miss.

AI can analyze massive amounts of financial data in real-time, spotting patterns, predicting cash flow, and even figuring out if Bob from Accounting is padding those expense reports. Companies that leverage AI aren't just saving time—they're making smarter financial decisions, reducing risk, and ensuring compliance without the headache.

### Why AI is Finance's New Best Friend

Finance professionals are already tapping into AI's power to automate processes, improve fraud detection, optimize investments, and sharpen risk analysis. Whether it's detecting sketchy transactions before they become a headline or forecasting cash flow with uncanny accuracy, AI is turning financial professionals into data-driven wizards.

**AI is helping finance teams:**

- **Automate the boring stuff:** AI can handle

bookkeeping, expense categorization, and invoice processing faster than you can say 'audit.'
- **Catch fraud before it happens:** AI scans financial data for anomalies and raises red flags before issues escalate.
- **Predict the future (sort of):** AI analyzes past trends and market conditions to improve forecasting, budgeting, and investment strategies.

With AI in finance, accountants sleep better at night, CFOs make more brilliant moves, and fraudsters have a harder time getting away with creative bookkeeping. If only AI could also figure out why office budgets always seem to disappear into 'miscellaneous expenses.'

### AI Adoption Trends in Finance & Accounting

- 75% of finance executives report using AI for risk assessment and fraud prevention.
- AI-powered automation can reduce financial reporting errors by 30%.
- AI-driven forecasting models improve accuracy by up to 20%.

### Key AI Tools for Finance & Accounting

#### AI-Powered Bookkeeping & Expense Management

**QuickBooks AI & Xero:** AI-powered bookkeeping that categorizes transactions and generates financial reports.

> ***Best Use:*** *Automating routine transaction categorization and reconciliation for small to medium businesses.*
> ***Watch Out For:*** *Still requires human oversight for complex accounting decisions and tax compliance.*

**Botkeeper:** AI-driven accounting automation for businesses.

> ***Best Use:*** *Scaling accounting operations without adding headcount in growing companies.*
> ***Watch Out For:*** *Implementation requires clean historical data and clearly defined accounting processes.*

**Expensify:** AI for automated expense tracking and receipt scanning.

> ***Best Use:*** *Streamlining employee expense reporting and approval workflows.*
> ***Watch Out For:*** *May need custom rule configuration to handle industry-specific expense policies.*

## AI for Fraud Detection & Risk Management

**Darktrace AI:** AI-driven fraud detection and cybersecurity analytics.

> ***Best Use:*** *Real-time monitoring of unusual financial transactions and network behavior.*
> ***Watch Out For:*** *Requires fine-tuning to reduce false positives in your specific business environment.*

**ThetaRay:** AI-powered risk assessment for financial

> *institutions.*
> ***Best Use:*** *Detecting money laundering and financial crime patterns across complex transaction networks.*
> ***Watch Out For:*** *An Advanced solution that requires specialized knowledge for implementation and management.*

**FICO Falcon Fraud Manager:** AI for detecting financial fraud patterns.

> ***Best Use:*** *Preventing payment fraud for credit card transactions and digital payments.*
> ***Watch Out For:*** *Needs regular model updates to stay ahead of evolving fraud techniques.*

### AI in Financial Forecasting & Business Strategy

**Kensho:** AI-driven financial analytics for investment insights.

- ***Best Use:*** *Analyzing vast financial datasets to identify market trends and investment opportunities.*
- ***Watch Out For:*** *A complex interface with a steep learning curve for non-technical financial analysts.*

**ZestFinance:** AI-powered credit risk assessment.

- ***Best Use:*** *Expanding credit access to underserved populations while maintaining risk controls.*
- ***Watch Out For:*** *Models require careful monitoring to ensure fair lending and avoid algorithmic bias.*

**Tesorio:** AI for cash flow forecasting and accounts receivable automation.

- ***Best Use:*** *Improving working capital management and predicting cash flow bottlenecks.*
- ***Watch Out For:*** *Effectiveness depends on the*

*quality of your historical payment and collection data.*

### Step-by-Step: Using AI for Financial Efficiency

### Scenario: AI-Driven Financial Management

- Automate bookkeeping with **QuickBooks AI**.
- Use **Expensify** to manage business expenses.
- Leverage **FICO Falcon** for fraud detection.
- Optimize investment decisions with **Kensho**.
- Implement AI forecasting models for financial planning.

### AI Best Practices for Finance Professionals

- Use AI for data-driven decision-making.
- Ensure compliance with financial regulations.
- Continuously monitor AI accuracy and bias.

### The Future of AI in Finance

- AI-driven investment advisors.
- Blockchain-integrated AI security.
- AI-powered tax optimization tools.

# AI FOR REAL ESTATE & PROPERTY MANAGEMENT

*How AI is Transforming Real Estate Transactions, Property Valuation, and Tenant Management*

## AI: The Smartest Real Estate Agent You'll Never Have to Pay Commission

Buying and selling real estate has always been a game of gut feelings, wild market swings, and the occasional questionable home appraisal (seriously, who decided that shag carpet adds value?). But AI is flipping the script, making real estate smarter, faster, and a whole lot less reliant on someone's uncle saying, "Trust me, this is a great deal."

AI-powered tools are revolutionizing everything from market analysis to property valuations, tenant management, and even maintenance predictions. Whether you're an investor, an agent, or a landlord tired of dealing with *mystery leaks* in rental units, AI is stepping in to optimize pricing, automate tenant interactions, and predict when the HVAC system is about to betray you.

## The Role of AI in Real Estate

AI is transforming the real estate industry by enabling professionals to predict market trends, automate property valuations, enhance customer service, and streamline property management. Gone are the days of relying on "gut instincts" and 20-page spreadsheets—AI crunches the data, identifies the trends, and enables real estate pros to make data-driven decisions that maximize profitability.

AI-powered analytics provide investors, agents, and property managers with deeper insights into fluctuating markets, ensuring they don't miss a golden opportunity (or accidentally overprice a house because it has "vintage charm," which often means no plumbing updates since 1972).

Integrating AI into real estate operations has led to faster sales cycles, better tenant experiences, and predictive maintenance that prevents disasters. From chatbots answering buyers' questions at 2 am to AI-powered algorithms determining the best time to buy or sell a property, AI is no longer a *nice-to-have* —it's the **secret weapon of modern real estate.**

### Key AI Tools for Real Estate & Property Management

**Best for:** Automating rent collection, tenant communications, and property maintenance, as well as estimating property values and predicting market trends.

**Limitations:** Initial setup and integration with existing systems may require time and resources. AI models may not always account for unique local factors affecting property prices.

### AI for Market Analysis & Property Valuation

**Zillow Zestimate:** AI-powered property valuation model analyzing historical and current market data.

> ***Best Use:*** *Quick comparative market analysis for residential properties in data-rich markets.*
> ***Watch Out For:*** *Accuracy varies significantly in*

*rural areas or unique properties with limited comparable sales.*

**HouseCanary:** AI-driven real estate forecasting and valuation platform.

***Best Use:*** *Investment portfolio analysis and identifying emerging neighborhood trends.*
***Watch Out For:*** *Premium pricing that may be cost-prohibitive for individual agents or small brokerages.*

**Reonomy:** AI-based commercial real estate market analysis.

***Best Use:*** *Uncovering off-market commercial investment opportunities and ownership research.*
***Watch Out For:*** *Data quality varies across different markets and property types.*

## AI-Powered Lead Generation & Client Management

***Best for:*** *Automating lead nurturing, improving client relationships.*
***Limitations:*** *AI recommendations require*

*human oversight to maintain personalized client engagement.*

**Rex AI:** AI-driven real estate CRM for personalized client recommendations.

***Best Use:*** *Creating tailored property matches based on client behavior and preferences.*
***Watch Out For:*** *Requires consistent data input to build accurate client profiles.*

**Follow Up Boss AI:** AI-assisted automated lead follow-ups.

***Best Use:*** *Maintaining engagement with long-term prospects without manual intervention.*
***Watch Out For:*** *Automated messages; they can feel impersonal if not properly customized.*

**OJO Labs:** AI chatbot for guiding homebuyers through the purchasing process.

***Best Use:*** *24/7 initial lead qualification and nurturing before agent involvement.*
***Watch Out For:*** *Complex buyer questions that may require human intervention—set clear handoff points.*

## AI for Property Management & Maintenance

**Entrata AI:** AI-powered property management software optimizing tenant interactions.

> ***Best Use:*** *Streamlining tenant communications and prioritizing maintenance requests.*
> ***Watch Out For:*** *Requires training staff on new workflows to fully realize efficiency gains.*

**AppFolio AI:** AI-enhanced rent collection and lease management.

> ***Best Use:*** *Automating payment reminders and processing to improve cash flow predictability.*
> ***Watch Out For:*** *Integration with existing accounting systems may require customization.*

**Bricks & Agent AI:** AI for predictive maintenance and smart home integration.

> ***Best Use:*** *Identifying maintenance issues before they become costly repairs.*
> ***Watch Out For:*** *Effectiveness depends on the quality of IoT sensors and connected devices in properties.*

## Step-by-Step: Using AI to Enhance Real Estate Operations

### Scenario: AI-Driven Real Estate Management

**1. Market Analysis & Property Pricing**

- Utilize **HouseCanary** to forecast pricing trends using comparable sales data.
- AI provides valuation estimates for properties based on location, demand, and recent transactions.

**2. Automating Lead Generation & Client Engagement**

- Implement the **OJO Labs** chatbot to qualify leads and answer client inquiries.
- Use **Follow Up Boss AI** to schedule and automate email follow-ups for potential buyers.

**3. Optimizing Property Listings**

- Use **Zillow's Zestimate** to determine the optimal listing price.
- AI analyzes the performance of previous listings to suggest the best times and marketing strategies for selling properties.

**4. Streamlining Property Management & Tenant Interactions**

- Use **Entrata AI** to automate rent collection and lease agreement processing.
- Implement **Bricks & Agent AI** to monitor maintenance requests and schedule proactive repairs.

## AI Best Practices for Real Estate Professionals

- Combine AI insights with human expertise when making property investment decisions.
- Use AI for lead generation while maintaining a personalized client experience.
- Regularly update AI models with local real estate trends to improve accuracy.
- Ensure compliance with fair housing regulations when using AI in property management.

## The Future of AI in Real Estate

- AI-driven smart contracts for seamless real estate transactions.
- Increased adoption of AI-based virtual property tours and augmented reality experiences.
- Predictive analytics is improving urban planning and housing development.

### Next Steps for Real Estate Professionals

- Choose an AI tool to test in your real estate operations.
- Evaluate how AI improves efficiency in property valuation and tenant management.
- Stay informed on AI trends shaping the future of real estate.

# AI FOR CUSTOMER SERVICE & SUPPORT

*How AI is Enhancing Customer Interactions, Automating Responses, and Improving Satisfaction*

## AI: Because Customer Service Reps Deserve a Break, Too

If you've ever had to call customer support and ended up screaming "REPRESENTATIVE!" into the void of an automated phone menu, you know just how painful lousy service can be. Enter AI—the tireless, patient, and slightly robotic customer service assistant that never gets annoyed, never puts you on hold, and (unfortunately) never laughs at your jokes.

AI isn't just about chatbots telling you to "restart your modem." It's revolutionizing how businesses handle inquiries, anticipate customer needs, and prevent customers from posting negative reviews on Twitter about their poor support experience. With AI-driven sentiment analysis, automated ticketing, and intelligent virtual assistants, companies can deliver faster, more personalized customer service—without exhausting human agents who have already answered, "Did you try turning it off and on again?" 47 times today.

### The Role of AI in Customer Service

AI is redefining customer service by improving response times, personalizing interactions, and automating routine inquiries. Businesses leveraging AI-powered chatbots, automated ticketing systems, and sentiment analysis can handle high volumes of customer interactions efficiently while maintaining a high level of service quality.

Companies using AI in customer service are seeing higher efficiency and happier customers. AI doesn't just answer

FAQs—it assists human agents by analyzing customer history, suggesting responses, and handling repetitive queries, freeing up teams to focus on complex or high-value interactions that require human judgment.

AI-powered tools also help companies anticipate customer needs, detect potential issues before they escalate, and provide 24/7 support without skyrocketing operational costs. Whether it's a chatbot that helps troubleshoot a product issue at 3 a.m. or AI flagging that a customer is *this close* to canceling their subscription, AI is turning customer service from reactive to proactive.

The result? Customers receive faster, better support, agents spend less time answering repetitive questions, and businesses streamline their entire customer service operation—without burning out their teams.

### Key AI Tools for Customer Service & Support

**Best for:** Reducing response times and managing high inquiry volumes.

**Limitations:** Chatbots may struggle with complex or nuanced customer concerns.

### AI Chatbots & Virtual Assistants

**Intercom AI:** AI-driven chatbot for automated customer interactions.

***Best Use:*** *Handling high-volume, routine inquiries and providing instant responses 24/7.*
***Watch Out For:*** *Requires thorough training on company-specific information to avoid generic responses.*

**Drift AI:** Conversational AI that assists in lead qualification and support.

***Best Use:*** *Converting website visitors into qualified leads while providing immediate support.*
***Watch Out For:*** *Conversation flows need regular optimization based on customer interaction patterns.*

**Zendesk AI:** AI-powered ticketing and response automation.

***Best Use:*** *Streamlining ticket categorization and suggesting responses to common questions.*
***Watch Out For:*** *Response suggestions may need customization to match your brand voice and policies.*

## AI for Sentiment Analysis & Customer Insights

> ***Best for:*** *Understanding customer sentiment and improving service strategies.*
> ***Limitations:*** *Requires integration with customer service platforms for optimal results.*

**HubSpot Service Hub:** AI-driven customer sentiment tracking.

> ***Best Use:*** *Monitoring customer satisfaction trends across all support channels.*
> ***Watch Out For:*** *Cultural and language nuances may affect sentiment accuracy in global operations.*

**MonkeyLearn:** AI-powered text analysis for customer feedback.

> ***Best Use:*** *Categorizing customer feedback from multiple sources to identify recurring issues.*
> ***Watch Out For:*** *Requires initial training periods to recognize industry-specific terminology.*

**IBM Watson:** Natural language processing for analyzing customer inquiries.

> ***Best Use:*** *Extracting actionable insights from*

*large volumes of unstructured customer communications.*

***Watch Out For:*** *An enterprise-level solution that may be complex to implement for smaller organizations.*

## AI for Workflow Automation & Ticket Management

***Best for:*** *Automating repetitive tasks and improving customer service efficiency.*

***Limitations:*** *May require manual intervention for nuanced support cases.*

**Freshdesk AI:** AI-powered ticket categorization and response prioritization.

***Best Use:*** *Automatically routing tickets to the correct department based on content analysis.*

***Watch Out For:*** *Rules require regular updates as product offerings and common issues evolve.*

**Ada AI:** Automates repetitive support queries and redirects complex cases to agents.

***Best Use:*** *Creating a seamless handoff between automated responses and human agents.*

> ***Watch Out For:*** *Transition points between AI and human support need careful design to avoid frustrating customers.*

**Zoho Desk AI:** AI-driven case routing and resolution recommendations.

> ***Best Use:*** *Providing agents with context-aware suggestions for faster problem resolution.*
> ***Watch Out For:*** *Agent adoption may require training and change management to leverage AI capabilities fully.*

**🛠 Tool Spotlight: Zoho CRM**
Affordable CRM platform with AI features for pipeline tracking, sales forecasting, and customer insights.
Learn more: zoho.com/crm

## Step-by-Step: Using AI to Improve Customer Support

### Scenario: AI-Driven Customer Service Enhancement

1. **Automating Customer Interactions**
    - Deploy **Intercom AI** to handle common inquiries such as FAQs and order status updates.
    - Train chatbots to deliver personalized responses tailored to customer profiles.
2. **Enhancing Sentiment Analysis**

    - Use **MonkeyLearn** to analyze customer sentiment from emails and support tickets.
    - Adjust customer service strategies based on insights into customer sentiment.
3. **Optimizing Ticket Management**
    - Implement **Freshdesk AI** to categorize and prioritize incoming customer issues.

Use **Zoho Desk AI** to route complex cases to specialized support agents.

### AI Best Practices for Customer Support Teams

- Train AI chatbots regularly to improve response accuracy.
- Combine AI insights with human customer service for high-value interactions.
- Monitor AI-driven interactions to prevent miscommunications or biases.
- Ensure AI adheres to data privacy and customer confidentiality standards.

### The Future of AI in Customer Service

- AI-powered voice assistants for real-time customer support.
- Predictive AI resolves customer issues before they occur.

- Enhanced AI-driven multilingual support for global businesses.

### Next Steps for Customer Service Professionals

- Select an AI tool to integrate into the customer support workflow. Assess AI's impact on response times and customer satisfaction.
- Stay updated on AI advancements that improve customer interactions.

# AI FOR MANUFACTURING & SUPPLY CHAIN MANAGEMENT

## How AI is Optimizing Production, Logistics, and Operational Efficiency

THIS CHAPTER PROVIDES MANUFACTURING AND SUPPLY CHAIN professionals with AI-driven solutions for improving operational efficiency, reducing costs, and optimizing logistics and production workflows.

### AI: Making Factories Smarter and Supply Chains Less of a Mess

Ah, supply chains—the unsung heroes of getting things where they need to go (until something goes wrong and suddenly, there's no toilet paper in sight). Manufacturing and logistics have always been fast-moving, high-stakes operations, and AI is stepping in to ensure that machines don't break down at the worst possible moment and that shipments arrive on time.

AI is bringing predictive maintenance, demand forecasting, and warehouse automation into the manufacturing and supply chain game. Instead of waiting for machines to fail, AI predicts issues before they happen. Instead of guessing how much inventory to stock, AI analyzes market trends and historical data to get it right. Instead of relying on gut feelings, AI ensures shipments are routed as efficiently as possible—because no one wants to explain why their product is still floating around in the Pacific.

### The Role of AI in Manufacturing & Supply Chain

AI is revolutionizing manufacturing and supply chain operations by increasing efficiency, reducing costs, and improving overall productivity. Whether it's keeping machines running smoothly, optimizing logistics, or preventing the dreaded "out of stock" notice, AI is helping manufacturers and logistics teams stay ahead of demand.

The adoption of AI enables companies to anticipate disruptions before they happen, optimize production schedules, and improve warehouse management. AI-powered automation in logistics and procurement ensures more accurate inventory tracking, faster delivery times, and fewer shipping nightmares.

**How AI is Making Supply Chains Smarter:**

- **Predictive maintenance** prevents factory shutdowns by spotting issues early.
- **AI-powered demand forecasting** helps companies stock what they need—no more over-ordering or panic shortages.
- **Automated quality control** detects defects before products leave the assembly line.
- **Smart logistics** optimizes delivery routes, cutting costs and reducing delays.

The result? Smoother production lines, faster shipping, fewer stock shortages, and far less human panic. AI is turning supply chains from "barely organized chaos" into a well-oiled, self-learning machine.

## Key AI Tools for Manufacturing & Supply Chain

### AI for Predictive Maintenance

**Best for:** Preventing equipment failures and reducing maintenance costs.

**Limitations:** Requires integration with IoT sensors and historical machine data.

**Uptake AI:** Uses machine learning to predict equipment failures before they happen.

> ***Best Use:*** *Extending the lifespan of critical production equipment while minimizing unplanned downtime.*
>
> ***Watch Out For:*** *Requires months of historical data to build accurate prediction models.*

**GE Predix:** AI-powered industrial analytics for optimizing machine performance.

> ***Best Use:*** *Comprehensive monitoring of complex industrial systems with multiple interdependent components.*
>
> ***Watch Out For:*** *Significant implementation costs and technical expertise required for full deployment.*

**SparkCognition:** AI-driven predictive maintenance to reduce downtime.

> ***Best Use:*** *Identifying subtle patterns in equipment data that human operators might miss.*
>
> ***Watch Out For:*** *Integration with legacy equipment may require additional sensors and hardware upgrades.*

**AI-Powered Demand Forecasting & Inventory Management**

**Best for:** Optimizing inventory levels and improving supply chain efficiency.

**Limitations:** Requires high-quality data inputs for accurate forecasting.

**Blue Yonder AI:** AI-driven supply chain planning and demand forecasting.

> ***Best Use:*** *Managing complex multi-echelon inventory systems with volatile demand patterns.*
>
> ***Watch Out For:*** *Algorithm training and fine-*

*tuning phase can take significant time before delivering optimal results.*

**IBM Sterling:** AI-powered inventory optimization and supply chain automation.

***Best Use:*** *End-to-end visibility across complex global supply chains with multiple partners.*
***Watch Out For:*** *Enterprise-level solution that requires coordinated implementation across departments.*

**o9 Solutions:** AI-based analytics for real-time demand forecasting.

***Best Use:*** *Integrating multiple demand signals (including social media and external events) for more accurate forecasts.*
***Watch Out For:*** *Requires high-quality master data and disciplined data governance practices.*

## AI for Quality Control & Production Optimization

**Best for:** Enhancing product quality and reducing production errors.

**Limitations:** Implementation may require specialized hardware and AI training.

**Landing AI:** AI-powered computer vision for detecting defects in manufacturing.

> ***Best Use:*** *Identifying subtle quality issues in high-speed production lines that human inspectors might miss.*
> ***Watch Out For:*** *Needs substantial examples of defects to train the system effectively.*

**Siemens MindSphere:** AI-driven, innovative manufacturing platform for process optimization.

> ***Best Use:*** *Comprehensive digital transformation of production processes with a focus on energy efficiency.*
> ***Watch Out For:*** *Works best with Siemens equipment; integration with other brands may be challenging.*

**Noodle.ai:** AI for improving factory efficiency and reducing waste.

> ***Best Use:*** *Identifying hidden inefficiencies in complex production processes and suggesting targeted improvements.*
> ***Watch Out For:*** *Requires clean operational data*

*and may initially surface more problems than expected.*

**AI in Logistics & Transportation**

**Best for:** Improving delivery efficiency and reducing logistics costs.

**Limitations:** Requires integration with transportation management systems.

**ClearMetal:** AI-powered supply chain visibility and logistics optimization.

> ***Best Use:*** *Improving delivery date accuracy and managing customer expectations in global shipping.*
> ***Watch Out For:*** *Benefits scale with the complexity of your supply chain; it may be overkill for simple logistics operations.*

**Flexport AI:** AI-driven freight forwarding and global shipping analytics.

> ***Best Use:*** *Optimizing international shipping routes and customs documentation for faster clearance.*

*Watch Out For: It still requires logistics expertise to interpret and implement AI recommendations.*

**FourKites:** AI-powered real-time shipment tracking and route optimization.

*Best Use: Providing customers with precise delivery windows and proactive delay notifications.*
*Watch Out For: Effectiveness depends on carrier participation and data sharing across your logistics network.*

🛠 **Tool Spotlight: FourKites**
Provides real-time shipment visibility, predictive ETAs, and analytics trusted by global carriers and shippers.
Learn more: fourkites.com

**Step-by-Step: Using AI to Improve Manufacturing & Supply Chain Operations**

**Scenario: AI-Driven Manufacturing & Logistics Optimization**

1. **Predictive Maintenance & Equipment Monitoring**
   - Use **Uptake AI** to detect potential failures in

machinery before they occur.

- AI alerts maintenance teams to schedule repairs proactively, reducing downtime.

2. **Optimizing Inventory Management & Demand Forecasting**
   - Deploy **Blue Yonder AI** to analyze market demand and predict inventory needs.
   - AI recommends stock adjustments to avoid shortages or overproduction.
3. **Automating Quality Control in Production**
   - Implement **Landing AI** to scan products for defects using computer vision.
   - AI flags defective items before they reach consumers, reducing returns and complaints.
4. **Enhancing Logistics & Supply Chain Efficiency**
   - Utilize **FourKites** for real-time tracking of shipments and route optimization.
   - AI-driven analytics predict delivery delays and suggest alternative routes.

## AI Best Practices for Manufacturing & Supply Chain Professionals

- Train AI models on historical data to improve accuracy in forecasting and maintenance.
- Integrate AI with IoT devices for real-time monitoring of production lines.
- Use AI-powered automation to reduce human error in logistics and warehouse management.

- Continuously assess AI model performance and update algorithms based on new data.

### The Future of AI in Manufacturing & Supply Chain

- AI-powered autonomous manufacturing systems with minimal human intervention.
- Blockchain-integrated AI for enhanced supply chain transparency and security.
- AI-driven sustainability solutions for optimizing energy and resource use.

### Next Steps for Manufacturing & Supply Chain Professionals

- Identify an AI tool to implement in manufacturing or supply chain workflows.
- Measure AI's impact on cost savings, efficiency, and production quality.
- Stay updated on advancements in AI-driven automation and logistics solutions.

# AI FOR NON-PROFITS & FUNDRAISING

*How AI is Transforming Donor Outreach, Fundraising, and Non-Profit Operations*

## AI: The Fundraising Intern Who Works 24/7 (And Never Asks for Free Snacks)

Running a non-profit is basically like juggling flaming torches while riding a unicycle—on a tightrope—over a pit of alligators. Early in my career, I was a Director for MDA, and there's never enough time, never enough money, and somehow, you still have to convince people to part with their cash for a good cause. I can't even imagine how much AI would have made the process easier. AI is the ever-efficient, tireless assistant that helps non-profits stretch every dollar, automate tedious admin work, and personalize donor outreach—all without once complaining about burnout.

AI is quickly becoming a game-changer for non-profits looking to optimize donor engagement, boost fundraising efforts, and streamline operations. With predictive analytics, AI can identify the most likely donors, craft personalized outreach campaigns, and even help with grant writing. Meanwhile, AI-powered automation ensures that staff spend less time on paperwork and more time making an impact.

## The Role of AI in Non-Profits & Fundraising

AI is transforming nonprofit work by automating repetitive tasks, enhancing donor outreach, and ensuring fundraising campaigns meet their goals. Whether it's automating donation tracking, writing grant proposals, or sending out personalized, data-driven donor messages that don't sound like generic spam, AI is making it easier for non-profits to do more with less.

With AI, non-profits can:

- **Find and keep high-value donors** using predictive analytics.
- **Automate repetitive administrative tasks** so staff can focus on making a real impact.
- **Optimize fundraising campaigns** with AI-generated outreach that converts.
- **Write stronger grant applications** (because AI doesn't procrastinate on deadlines).

Gone are the days of throwing fundraising emails into the void and hoping for the best. AI analyzes donor behavior, refines messaging, and helps non-profits build stronger, long-term relationships with supporters. The result? More funds raised, less burnout, and a lot fewer sleepless nights for non-profit teams.

### Key AI Tools for Non-Profits & Fundraising

#### AI for Donor Outreach & Fundraising Campaigns

**Best for:** Identifying high-value donors, improving fundraising campaigns.
**Limitations:** Requires accurate historical donor data for best results.

**DonorPerfect AI:** AI-driven donor analytics predicting who is most likely to give and when. donorperfect.com

> ***Best Use:*** *Targeting seasonal campaigns to the most receptive donor segments based on giving history.*
> ***Watch Out For:*** *Smaller organizations may not have enough donor data to generate meaningful predictions.*

**Gravyty:** AI-powered donor retention and personalized outreach. Gravyty.com

> ***Best Use:*** *Creating personalized stewardship plans for mid-level donors who might upgrade to major gifts.*
> ***Watch Out For:*** *AI-generated outreach suggestions still need personalization to avoid sounding generic.*

**Virtuous CRM:** AI-enhanced donor relationship management with automation capabilities. Virtuous.org

> ***Best Use:*** *Building comprehensive donor profiles that capture both online and offline engagement.*
> ***Watch Out For:*** *Staff training requirements to fully utilize the platform's AI capabilities.*

. . .

## AI for Grant Writing & Proposal Automation

**Best for:** Saving time on grant applications, improving funding success rates.
**Limitations:** AI-generated drafts still require human refinement for mission alignment.

**ChatGPT for Grant Writing:** AI-assisted drafting of grant applications and funding proposals.

> ***Best Use:*** *Generating first drafts of program descriptions and impact statements that can be refined.*
> ***Watch Out For:*** *AI may miss nuanced grant requirements without specific prompting and oversight.*

**Instrumental AI:** AI-driven grant discovery, matching non-profits with the right opportunities. Instrumentl.com

**Best Use:** Identifying specialized funding opportunities that align with your organization's mission.

> ***Watch Out For:*** *Most valuable for organizations with dedicated grant writing staff who can act on opportunities.*

**Grantable AI:** AI-generated first drafts of grant applications, reducing manual writing time .grantable.co

**Best Use:** Repurposing successful grant language across multiple applications to maintain consistency.

> ***Watch Out For:*** *Not a replacement for understanding funder priorities and crafting tailored applications.*

**AI for Back-Office & Administrative Automation**

**Best for:** Reducing manual work, improving operational efficiency.
**Limitations:** Requires integration with existing non-profit software.

**UiPath:** AI-powered automation for processing donations, payroll, and compliance paperwork.

> ***Best Use:*** *Automating repetitive data entry tasks to free up staff for mission-focused work.*
> ***Watch Out For:*** *Implementation requires technical expertise that many non-profits may not have in-house.*

**Zapier AI:** Workflow automation between donor databases, email marketing tools, and finance software.

> ***Best Use:*** *Creating seamless data flows between different systems without custom development.*
> ***Watch Out For:*** *Monthly subscription costs can add up based on the number of automations and tasks.*

**Hootsuite AI:** AI-driven social media management to schedule posts and optimize engagement.

> ***Best Use:*** *Maintaining a consistent social media presence with a limited communications staff.*
> ***Watch Out For:*** *Less effective for organizations where real-time community engagement is critical.*

## Step-by-Step: Using AI to Boost Non-Profit Efficiency

## Scenario: AI-Powered Fundraising & Donor Engagement

1. **Identifying High-Value Donors**
    - Use **DonorPerfect AI** to analyze past giving patterns and predict future donations.

    - AI prioritizes potential donors based on their engagement levels and giving history.
2. **Automating Personalized Donor Outreach**
    - Deploy **Gravyty** to send AI-personalized email and text campaigns.
    - AI adapts messaging based on donor behavior and past interactions.
3. **Streamlining Grant Writing**
    - Use **ChatGPT for Grant Writing** to generate a first draft of a funding proposal.
    - AI cross-references grant guidelines to ensure compliance with application requirements.
4. **Optimizing Social Media & Marketing**
    - Implement **Hootsuite AI** to schedule and analyze social media campaigns.
    - AI suggests best posting times and formats to maximize donor engagement.

### AI Best Practices for Non-Profit Leaders

- Balance AI automation with human relationships—donors want to feel valued, not like they're talking to a robot.
- Use AI insights to enhance storytelling and messaging impact, not to replace authentic communication.
- Continuously train AI tools with updated donor data to improve accuracy.
- Ensure compliance with the ethical use of AI,

particularly in data privacy and donor information security.

### The Future of AI in Non-Profits & Fundraising

- AI-powered voice assistants are helping donors complete pledges in seconds.
- Predictive AI identifying trends in philanthropy and emerging donor segments.
- AI-driven automation reduces overhead costs, allowing non-profits to allocate more funds directly to their causes.

### Next Steps for Non-Profit Professionals

- Test an AI tool in donor outreach or grant writing to assess the efficiency gains it can provide.
- Monitor AI's impact on fundraising success and engagement metrics.
- Stay updated on AI-driven innovations that can help stretch non-profit resources further.

# AI FOR E-LEARNING

## How AI is Transforming Learning, Teaching, and Student Engagement

E-LEARNING HAS EXPLODED IN RECENT YEARS, TURNING THE internet into a giant, global classroom where students can learn anything from astrophysics to how to fold a fitted sheet (finally). But let's face it—not all online courses are created equal. Some are engaging and interactive, while others feel like watching paint dry. That's where AI comes in.

AI is personalizing online learning, automating assessments, and making virtual education more interactive than ever before. Whether it's adaptive learning platforms that adjust to student progress or AI tutors that answer questions in real time, AI is bridging the gap between traditional education and digital learning.

## The Role of AI in E-Learning

AI is transforming online education by making courses more engaging, interactive, and tailored to each learner's needs. Whether it's an online university program, a corporate training course, or a YouTube tutorial on quantum physics, AI is enhancing digital learning experiences at every level.

With AI in e-learning, students can:

- **Access AI-driven tutoring** that provides real-time assistance.
- **Receive personalized lesson recommendations** based on learning patterns.
- **Use AI-powered assessments** that provide instant feedback.
- **Engage with interactive AI chatbots** that keep learning dynamically and are fun.

For educators and course creators, AI helps optimize content delivery, automate administrative tasks, and improve learner engagement—because no one wants to sit through another dry, monotonous slideshow.

### The Best AI Tools for E-Learning

#### AI for Personalized Learning & Tutoring

**Squirrel AI** – Adaptive learning platform adjusting content based on student progress.

> ***Best Use:*** *Identifying knowledge gaps and creating customized learning paths for students struggling with specific concepts.*
> ***Watch Out For:*** *Requires significant data collection to be effective—privacy concerns should be addressed.*

**Carnegie Learning** – AI-powered tutoring for math and science subjects.

> ***Best Use:*** *Providing step-by-step problem-solving assistance for complex STEM concepts and offering immediate feedback.*
> ***Watch Out For:*** *Works best when integrated with in-person instruction rather than as a standalone solution.*

**Khan Academy's Khanmigo** – AI-based virtual tutor for interactive, personalized learning.

> ***Best Use:*** *Supplemental AI tutoring for students who need extra help outside of classroom hours.*
>
> ***Watch Out For:*** *Not a replacement for real human guidance and may not adapt well to highly creative or subjective subjects.*

**Socratic (by Google)** – AI-powered educational search tool that helps students get instant answers with explanations for homework questions.

> ***Best Use:*** *Providing just-in-time help when students are stuck on specific homework problems.*
>
> ***Watch Out For:*** *Students might rely on quick answers rather than developing problem-solving skills.*

### AI for Automated Grading & Assessments

**Gradescope AI** – AI-driven automated grading for assignments and exams.

> ***Best Use:*** *Teachers who want to cut grading time*

*in half while providing consistent feedback across large numbers of students.*

**Watch Out For:** *AI can misinterpret creative answers or nuanced arguments—manual review is still needed for complex assessments.*

**Turnitin AI** – AI-powered plagiarism detection and writing analysis.

**Best Use:** *Academic integrity enforcement in online courses where verification can be challenging.*

**Watch Out For:** *False positives happen, so constantly review flagged content before taking action against students.*

**Quizlet AI** – AI-generated quizzes and flashcards for student engagement.

**Best Use:** *Helping students reinforce knowledge through active recall and spaced repetition techniques.*

**Watch Out For:** *AI-generated questions can sometimes oversimplify concepts or focus too heavily on memorization rather than understanding.*

## AI for Course Content Optimization

**Ellucian AI** – AI-powered student information system for higher education.

> ***Best Use:*** *Streamlining administrative processes and providing personalized communication with students about important deadlines and requirements.*
>
> ***Watch Out For:*** *Implementation can be complex and requires significant institutional buy-in to be effective.*

**Salesforce for Education** – AI-driven CRM for student recruitment and engagement.

> ***Best Use:*** *Creating targeted outreach campaigns and predicting which prospective students are most likely to enroll and succeed.*
>
> ***Watch Out For:*** *Risk of over-automation—personal touch points still matter in education.*

**IBM Watson Education** – AI-powered predictive analytics for student performance monitoring.

> ***Best Use:*** *Early identification of at-risk students and providing targeted interventions before they fall behind.*

*Watch Out For: Algorithmic bias can affect predictions—regularly audit the system to ensure fair treatment of all student populations.*

**AI in E-Learning: Real-World Scenarios**

**Scenario 1: AI-Enhanced Virtual Classroom**

**Challenge:** A university needed to transition 200+ courses online during the pandemic while maintaining student engagement and academic rigor.

**AI Solution:** Implemented an AI-powered virtual classroom platform combining adaptive learning algorithms with real-time analytics.

**Results:**

- Student completion rates increased by 28% compared to standard online courses.
- AI-generated personalized learning paths based on assessment performance
- Automated plagiarism detection and proctoring reduced academic integrity violations by 65%
- Faculty time spent on administrative tasks decreased by 40%

**Key Takeaway:** AI's ability to personalize content delivery and automate assessment enabled a more engaging online learning experience that rivaled traditional classroom outcomes.

**Scenario 2: Corporate Training Transformation**

**Challenge:** A global corporation struggled with low completion rates and knowledge retention in mandatory compliance training.

**AI Solution:** Replaced static e-learning modules with an AI-driven microlearning platform that adapted to each employee's knowledge gaps and learning preferences.

**Results:**

- Training completion rates jumped from 62% to 94%
- Knowledge retention (measured through assessments) improved by 41%
- AI chatbot answered 24/7 policy questions, reducing HR inquiries by 35%
- Training time decreased by 28% while maintaining certification requirements

**Key Takeaway:** AI-powered personalization transformed mandatory training from a tedious checkbox exercise into an efficient, engaging learning experience.

**Scenario 3: Language Learning Revolution**

**Challenge:** A language education platform sought to improve conversation practice and pronunciation feedback without increasing human tutoring costs.

**AI Solution:** Implemented an AI conversation partner with voice recognition, real-time pronunciation correction, and adaptive dialogue generation.

**Results:**

- Students increased practice time by 3x compared to traditional self-study methods.
- AI provided instant feedback on 15,000+ pronunciation attempts daily
- Learning algorithms adapt conversation difficulty based on learner progress
- Student proficiency advancement accelerated by 40%

**Key Takeaway:** AI enables practice opportunities that would be financially impossible to provide through human tutors alone, dramatically scaling personalized feedback.

## Best Practices for Implementing AI in E-Learning

### Balance AI and Human Elements

*Do: Use AI for personalization, feedback, and content delivery while preserving human connection through live sessions, instructor feedback, and peer collaboration.*

*Don't: Replace all human interactions with AI elements. Students still need social learning and mentorship from real instructors.*

### Focus on Ethical Data Collection

*Do: Be transparent about what learner data is collected, how it's used, and implement strong privacy protections.*

*Don't: Gather excessive data or use learning analytics in ways students haven't consented to. Avoid tracking outside the learning environment.*

### Design for Accessibility and Inclusion

*Do: Ensure AI tools work effectively for students with disabilities and diverse learning needs —test systems with diverse user groups.*

*Don't: Implement AI systems that create new barriers or bias against specific student populations. Regularly audit for algorithmic fairness.*

### Implement Gradual Integration

***Do:*** *Start with focused AI applications in areas of greatest need, gather feedback, and expand strategically.*
***Don't:*** *Overwhelm faculty or students with too many AI tools at once. Avoid technology for technology's sake.*

### Prioritize Skill Development, Not Just Content Delivery

***Do:*** *Design AI interactions that promote critical thinking, problem-solving, and metacognitive skills.*
***Don't:*** *Create systems that deliver information or provide answers without developing a more profound understanding.*

### Establish Clear AI Boundaries

***Do:*** *Create clear policies regarding appropriate AI use by students. Distinguish between AI as a learning aid versus academic dishonesty.*
***Don't:*** *Leave AI use policies ambiguous, forcing*

*students to guess what constitutes appropriate assistance.*

## The Future of AI in E-Learning: What's Next

### Emerging Trends to Watch

- **Immersive AI-Powered Learning Environments**
    - Virtual and augmented reality environments with AI-guided instruction will create immersive simulations for skills that traditionally required physical practice—from medical procedures to complex equipment operation.
- **Emotional Intelligence in Learning Systems**
    - Next-generation AI will detect learner frustration, confusion, or disengagement through facial recognition, voice analysis, and interaction patterns, adapting content delivery in response to emotional states.
- **Hyper-Personalized Learning Pathways**
    - AI will move beyond adapting content difficulty to creating unique learning journeys based on career goals, learning preferences, strengths, and weaknesses—essentially a personal curriculum designer for every student.
- **AI-Generated Content and Curriculum**
    - AI will create customized learning materials on demand, generating explanations, examples,

and practice activities tailored to specific learner needs and interests.

- **Predictive Skills Mapping**
    - AI systems will analyze labor market trends and individual learner profiles to recommend specific skills development pathways aligned with emerging career opportunities.

**Getting Started with AI in E-Learning**

1. **Audit Current Pain Points:** Identify specific challenges in your existing e-learning offerings that AI could address.
2. **Start Small:** Begin with focused implementations like an AI chatbot for common questions or automated feedback on specific assessment types.
3. **Measure Impact:** Establish clear metrics for success and track outcomes after AI implementation.
4. **Gather User Feedback:** Collect insights from both instructors and learners about their experience with AI tools.
5. **Develop AI Literacy:** Invest in training for educators and instructional designers to understand AI capabilities and limitations.

The future of e-learning isn't just about automation—it's about augmentation. AI will enhance human educators' abilities to deliver personalized, engaging learning experiences at scale, allowing teachers to focus on what they do best: inspiring, mentoring, and providing the human connection that remains at the heart of effective education.

# ETHICAL CONSIDERATIONS—SELLING RESPONSIBLY WITH AI

*"Ethics are very important to me."*

Let's have an uncomfortable conversation, shall we? The kind that makes you squirm a little in your seat but leaves you better for having endured it—like a necessary dental cleaning or that long-overdue talk with your teenager about their "interesting" music choices.

We've spent ten chapters exploring all the fantastic ways AI can supercharge your sales process, boost your productivity, and potentially make you rich enough to finally buy that vacation home you've been eyeing on Zillow during boring conference calls. (Don't worry, I do it too. My fantasy island is getting more remote with every price increase in the housing market.)

But here's the sobering reality check we need: with great AI power comes great responsibility. And if sci-fi movies have taught us anything, it's that skipping the "responsibility" part typically ends with robots hunting humans through abandoned shopping malls. While your AI sales tools are unlikely to become sentient and overthrow civilization, they can certainly cause harm if deployed carelessly.

I learned this lesson the painful way. Early in my AI adoption journey, I was so excited about our new automated email personalization system that I rushed it into production without proper testing. The result? Our system sent emails addressing a major healthcare client as "Dear [First Name]"—but filled the rest of the message with details from a completely different customer in the same industry. That's right—we accidentally shared confidential information across companies because I was too eager to show off our shiny new AI toy.

The ensuing damage control took weeks, and we nearly lost both accounts. Worse yet, the trust we'd carefully built with these clients evaporated in a single careless moment.

So before you rush headlong into the AI sales revolution, let's talk about how to harness these powerful tools ethically and responsibly. Because sustainable success isn't just about having the most advanced technology—it's about using it in ways that maintain trust, respect privacy, and create genuine value for everyone involved.

**Why Ethics Matter in AI-Powered Sales (Even When No One's Looking)**

Ethics in AI sales isn't just about avoiding PR disasters or legal penalties (though those are certainly motivating factors). It's fundamentally about creating sustainable business relationships in a world where customers are increasingly savvy about—and sensitive to—how their data is used.

Consider these revealing statistics:

- 86% of consumers say transparency is more important than ever before
- 75% of consumers won't buy from companies they don't trust to protect their data
- 71% of consumers would stop doing business with a company if it shared their sensitive data without permission
- Companies that experience data ethics scandals

see an average 7% drop in stock price and can take up to a year to recover reputation metrics.

Beyond the numbers, there's the simple human element: how would you feel if you discovered a company was using your data in ways you hadn't consented to? Or if an AI system was making critical decisions about your account without transparency or recourse? Or if you learned that a personalized message was generated by a machine pretending to be human?

The golden rule applies here—sell to others as you would want to be sold to. And I'm fairly certain that none of us aspire to be manipulated, deceived, or have our privacy violated in the name of someone else's commission check.

I've watched companies take radically different approaches to AI ethics, with predictably different outcomes:

**Company A** viewed ethics as an annoying compliance checkbox. They used AI to scrape data from various sources, generated personalized messages at scale, and trained their system on biased historical data that perpetuated existing inequities. Their short-term metrics looked great...until the lawsuits started, their reputation imploded, and customers fled. Their CEO told me, "We'll worry about ethics once we're profitable." They never reached profitability.

**Company B** incorporated ethics into its AI strategy from the outset. They obtained proper permissions for data use, maintained transparency about when AI was being used versus when humans were, and regularly audited their systems for bias. Their growth was perhaps slightly slower initially, but they built lasting trust that translated into exceptional retention and word-of-mouth. Five years later, they're thriving while Company A is a business school case study in what not to do.

The lesson? Ethical AI isn't just morally right—it's commercially astute. Let's examine the key principles that should guide your AI sales strategies.

**Essential Ethical Principles for AI-Powered Sales**

Here are the foundational ethical principles every sales organization should consider when implementing AI—along with practical guidance on how to live by them (because principles without practices are just fancy wall decorations).

**Transparency and Honesty**

- **The Principle:** Be transparent with customers about when and how you're using AI in your sales process. Don't pretend AI-generated content is human-created, and don't hide algorithmic decision-making that impacts customers.
- **Practical Application:** • disclose when chatbots or

AI assistants are engaging with customers • When sending AI-generated emails, either acknowledge the AI assistance or have a human review and take ownership of the content • Explain the factors that influence AI-based decisions about accounts (like lead scoring or discount eligibility)

*My guideline*: I follow what I call the "Mom Test"—if my mom would feel deceived or manipulated by how we're using AI, then we need to reconsider our approach. (My mother has an uncanny ability to detect BS, so this is a high bar in my case.)

**Data Privacy and Consent**

- **The Principle:** Respect customer data by obtaining proper consent, using information only for intended purposes, and maintaining robust security practices.
- **Practical Application:** • Implement proper data governance frameworks that track consent for every data point you collect • Use AI tools like **ContextMinds** and **Perplexity** for research without exposing confidential customer information • Regularly audit your data handling practices with tools like Originality.ai to prevent unintended exposure

*Embarrassing confession*: Before I got serious about data privacy, I once uploaded our entire prospect database to test a new AI tool—without reading the fine print that the company could use this data to train their models. Essentially, I gave away our valuable prospect information for free. Lesson painfully learned: always understand the data policies of any AI service you use.

**Fairness and Non-Discrimination**

> **The Principle:** Ensure your AI systems don't perpetuate or amplify biases that disadvantage certain groups based on protected characteristics like race, gender, age, or disability.
>
> **Practical Application:** • Regularly test AI-generated content for bias, especially in personalization algorithms • Avoid training AI exclusively on historical sales data if your past customers lack diversity • Implement fairness metrics in your lead scoring and opportunity ranking systems

***Game-changing approach***: One FinTech company I worked with discovered that their AI lead scoring model systematically undervalued small businesses owned by women and minorities—not because of any explicit bias, but because their historical sales data reflected decades of industry bias. They rebuilt their model with adjusted parameters and discovered an entire segment of highly valuable customers they had been overlooking. Their more ethical approach opened new market opportunities.

**Human Oversight and Intervention**

- **The Principle:** Maintain meaningful human oversight of AI systems, particularly for decisions that have significant consequences for customers.
- **Practical Application:** • Establish clear thresholds for when AI recommendations require human review • Create accessible appeals processes for customers who want to challenge AI-driven decisions • Regularly audit AI outputs for quality, compliance, and ethical considerations

***The difference it makes***: My team implemented a "confidence threshold" rule—our AI could automatically execute recommendations when its confidence score exceeded 85%, but required human review for anything below that threshold. This simple guardrail prevented many potential mistakes while still capturing most of the efficiency benefits. When a major prospect was incorrectly flagged as low-value by our system (due to missing key contextual information), our human review caught the error before any damage was done.

**Value Creation over Exploitation**

- **The Principle:** Use AI to create genuine value for customers, not just to extract more value from them through manipulation or pressure tactics.
- **Practical Application:** • Focus AI implementations on solving customer problems,

not just optimizing for short-term sales metrics • Test AI-driven approaches against the question: "Does this help the customer make a better decision for their needs?" • Measure long-term satisfaction and value metrics, not just conversion rates

***Personal revelation***: I once implemented an AI system that optimized email send times for maximum open rates. It worked brilliantly—open rates increased by 37%! But when we dug deeper, we discovered it was essentially catching people at their most vulnerable moments (late at night, early Sunday mornings) when their decision-making might be compromised. The engagement was higher, but it felt predatory. We adjusted the system to optimize for response quality, not just open rates, which better aligned with genuine value creation.

## Real-World Ethical Dilemmas in AI Sales (And How to Navigate Them)

Let's explore some common ethical dilemmas that arise when implementing AI in sales processes—and practical approaches to handling them responsibly.

### Dilemma #1: The Personalization vs. Privacy Paradox

- **The Scenario:** Your AI can create hyper-personalized outreach by analyzing prospects' social media activity, online behavior, and personal details—resulting in significantly higher engagement rates. But this level of personalization can feel invasive or creepy when recipients realize how much you know about them.

- **Ethical Approach:** • Establish clear boundaries for personalization—information shared publicly in a professional context is generally fair game; personal details from private accounts usually aren't
    - Test personalization against the "surprise factor"—would the prospect be surprised to learn how you got this information? If so, reconsider using it
    - •Be transparent about the source of your information when appropriate ("I noticed on your company blog that you're expanding into healthcare...")

***My guideline***: I use what I call the "coffee meeting rule"—if it would be weird to mention something in a first casual business meeting, it's probably too personal for AI-driven outreach. For example, saying their company's recent product launch is fine; referencing their child's soccer tournament from Instagram is not.

### Dilemma #2: AI-Generated Communication Transparency

- **The Scenario:** Your team is using AI to generate personalized emails, proposals, and even conversation talking points at scale. These materials sound authentically human and drive excellent results. Should you disclose AI helped create them?
- **Ethical Approach:** • Consider the context and degree of AI involvement—fully automated messages with no human oversight deserve different treatment than AI-assisted content that a human has reviewed and owns
  - When in doubt, err on the side of transparency without overcomplicating the issue
  - Focus on the value being provided rather than the technology behind it

***Real-world solution***: We implemented a simple practice for our AI-generated emails. If a human meaningfully reviewed and edited the content before sending, no special disclosure was needed (it's just another writing tool at that point, like spell-check). For fully automated messages with minimal human oversight, we included a subtle but clear disclosure: "This personalized message was crafted with assistance from our AI tools, but our commitment to your success is 100% human." Surprisingly, this transparency improved response rates—people appreciated the honesty.

. . .

### Dilemma #3: Algorithmic Bias in Lead Scoring and Forecasting

- **The Scenario:** Your AI-powered lead scoring system is demonstrating concerning patterns—it seems to systematically undervalue certain types of prospects based on characteristics that could correlate with protected attributes (even though those attributes aren't directly included in the model).
- **Ethical Approach:** • Implement regular bias audits of your AI systems, checking for disparate outcomes across different demographic groups
  - Use techniques like "fairness through awareness" where you deliberately balance your training data to counteract historical biases
  - Consider multiple definitions of fairness and make conscious choices about which to prioritize

***Game-changing approach***: A B2B software company discovered its AI was assigning lower lead scores to companies with predominantly female leadership teams—not because gender was an input, but because it had learned from historical data where the sales team had preferentially pursued male-led companies. They addressed this by balancing their training data and adding a regular fairness audit. Within six months, they had increased their customer diversity and discovered an untapped market segment with excellent conversion rates.

**Dilemma #4: The Automation vs. Employment Balance**

- **The Scenario**: Your new AI sales tools could automate significant portions of your SDR or BDR roles, potentially leading to staff reductions. How do you balance efficiency with responsibility to your team?
- **Ethical Approach:** • Focus first on automating the repetitive, low-value tasks that salespeople generally dislike
  - Invest in reskilling programs that help your team work alongside AI rather than be replaced by it
  - Be transparent with your team about automation plans and involve them in implementation

***The human-centered solution***: One tech company I advised took an innovative approach to this dilemma. Instead of reducing headcount when they implemented advanced automation, they redeployed their SDRs to more strategic, consultative roles. They invested in training programs that taught their team how to use the AI tools effectively and focus on higher-value activities. The result? Their cost-per-acquisition decreased while employee satisfaction increased dramatically. They discovered that human-AI teams outperformed either humans or AI working alone.

## Practical Framework for Ethical AI Decision-Making in Sales

Beyond specific scenarios, you need a repeatable process for making ethical decisions about AI implementation. Here's a simple framework I've found effective:

### 1. Identify Stakeholders and Impacts

Before implementing any AI sales tool or process, systematically identify all stakeholders who might be affected and consider potential impacts:

- Sales team members
- Your broader organization
- Customers and prospects
- Partners and suppliers
- Society at large.

***My approach***: I create a simple stakeholder impact grid for each AI initiative, mapping both intended benefits and potential risks for each group. This helps identify ethical concerns early and ensures we're not unquestioningly optimizing for one stakeholder at the expense of others.

### 2. Apply Ethical Principles and Balance Tradeoffs

Evaluate the initiative against core ethical principles and acknowledge that sometimes these principles may conflict, requiring thoughtful balancing:

- Would this approach pass the transparency test with all stakeholders?
- Are we respecting data privacy and consent?
- Have we tested for and mitigated potential biases?
- • Is there appropriate human oversight?
- Does this create genuine value rather than exploit vulnerabilities?

*Lesson learned*: Achieving perfect ethical purity is rarely attainable in complex business environments. The goal is to make conscious, defensible choices rather than accidentally stumbling into ethical problems. I've found that simply documenting our ethical reasoning creates accountability and leads to better decisions.

### 3. Implement Safeguards and Monitoring

Once you've proceeded with an AI implementation, establish guardrails:

- Clear usage guidelines and boundary conditions
- Regular auditing and testing protocols

- Feedback mechanisms for concerns or issues
- Continuous monitoring for unexpected consequences

*Game-changing approach*: One healthcare technology company created an "AI Ethics Committee" that included sales team members, technical staff, and customer representatives. This cross-functional group reviewed AI implementations, established monitoring metrics, and had the authority to recommend modifications when ethical concerns arose. This distributed responsibility for ethical AI across the organization rather than isolating it in a compliance function.

**4. Learn, Adapt, and Improve**

Ethical AI requires continuous learning and evolution:

- Schedule regular reviews of AI systems and their impacts
- Stay updated on evolving ethical standards and best practices
- Encourage a culture where ethical concerns can be raised without fear
- Be willing to modify or abandon approaches that create unexpected ethical issues.

*Personal confession*: My biggest ethical failures with AI haven't come from malicious intent but from simple inability to revisit systems after implementation. An email personalization system that worked beautifully at launch gradually became problematic as it accumulated biases from interaction data. We now have a calendar for mandatory quarterly ethical reviews of all our AI systems—even the ones that seem to be working perfectly.

**Mini Training Opportunity: Ethical AI Role-Playing**

Here's a valuable exercise for your team to build ethical AI muscles:

Create scenario cards describing realistic AI ethics dilemmas in sales, such as:

- You discover your AI lead scoring seems biased against smaller companies
- Your automated email system is generating misleading content
- A customer asks if they've been communicating with a real person or AI
- Have team members take turns drawing scenarios and discussing:

- What ethical principles are at stake in this situation?
- What are the short-term business implications of different responses?
- What are the long-term relationship and reputation implications?
- What would be the most ethical approach, and how would you implement it?

This exercise builds ethical reasoning skills in a safe environment before real situations arise. I've found it particularly effective to run these sessions with diverse participants—salespeople, technical team members, and customer advocates often have different perspectives that enrich the discussion.

### Beyond Compliance: Building an Ethical AI Culture in Sales

Ethical AI isn't achieved through a checklist or policy document—it requires building a culture where ethical considerations are woven into everyday decision-making. Here are practical ways to cultivate this culture:

***Lead by Example:*** *Leadership must show a commitment to ethical AI principles, even when it creates short-term challenges or costs.*

**Personal standard:** *I make a point of publicly*

*acknowledging when we've made ethically questionable decisions with our AI systems and how we're addressing them. This psychological safety encourages others to raise concerns early rather than hiding problems.*

***Reward Ethical Behavior:** Recognize and celebrate team members who identify ethical issues or suggest more responsible approaches.*

**Real example***: One company I worked with incorporated "ethical AI implementation" into their sales team's performance reviews and bonus calculations. A salesperson who identified a bias in their lead scoring algorithm received recognition equal to that of their top performers. This sent a powerful message about what the organization truly valued.*

***Provide Ethical AI Training:** Ensure your team understands both the technical and ethical dimensions of the AI tools they're using.*

**Practical approach***: We created a simple "AI Ethics Passport" training program that every team member must complete before gaining access to our AI sales tools. It covered basic principles, common scenarios, and clear* *guidelines for escalating concerns. This baseline knowledge ensured that everyone understood their responsibilities for the ethical use of AI.*

***Create Clear Escalation Paths:*** *Ensure team members can raise ethical concerns without fear of retaliation.*

**The structure that works:** *We established a simple "AI Ethics Hotline" where any team member could report concerns anonymously. More importantly, we tracked and published the outcomes of these reports, demonstrating that raising ethical issues led to positive changes rather than being lost in a black hole.*

## Ethical Risks of Advanced AI

As we consider the ethical implementation of AI in sales, it's worth acknowledging the broader concerns about AI's advancement. Recent expert warnings suggest that Artificial General Intelligence (AGI) could pose serious risks as early as 2026, with systems capable of manipulation, deception, or gaining control over critical infrastructure.

While these existential concerns may seem distant from your day-to-day sales operations, they underscore why ethical considerations aren't just nice-to-have—they're essential. The AI tools we use in sales today are laying the foundation for tomorrow's more advanced systems. By establishing ethical guardrails now in our relatively simple applications, we help shape the development path for more sophisticated AI to come.

This isn't about fear-mongering—it's about responsible stewardship. The small decisions we make today regarding transparency, data usage, and human oversight significantly contribute to the development of the broader AI ecosystem. By being ethical AI practitioners in sales, we're doing our part to ensure that more advanced iterations develop along responsible, human-centered paths.

**Big Picture**

Ethical AI isn't just a nice-to-have or a compliance checkbox—it's the foundation for sustainable success in an increasingly AI-driven sales landscape. By embracing transparency, respecting privacy, ensuring fairness, maintaining human oversight, and focusing on genuine value creation, you can harness AI's incredible potential while avoiding the pitfalls that have damaged so many organizations.

The companies that thrive in the long term won't just be

those with the most advanced AI capabilities—they'll be those who use AI responsibly to create authentic connections and deliver real value. Ethics and effectiveness aren't competing priorities; they're complementary forces that together create truly sustainable sales success.

In our next chapter, we'll explore how to future-proof your sales career in an age of rapid AI advancement. We'll examine strategies for continuously adapting your skills, staying ahead of technological changes, and positioning yourself as a valued expert who leverages AI as a tool rather than being replaced by it.

And remember—the goal isn't to be perfect in your AI ethics approach. It's to be thoughtful, intentional, and continuously improving. That you're reading this chapter puts you ahead of many organizations that rush into AI implementation without considering the ethical implications. Keep asking the hard questions, even when no one else is, and you'll not only sell more effectively—you'll sleep better at night.

**Quick Recap:**

- The ethical implementation of AI directly impacts business success through trust, reputation, and sustainable relationships.
- Key ethical principles include transparency, data

privacy, fairness, human oversight, and genuine value creation.

- Common dilemmas include the balance between personalization/privacy, the disclosure of AI-generated content, algorithmic bias, and the impact of automation on employment.
- A practical ethical framework involves identifying stakeholders, applying principles, implementing safeguards, and continuous improvement.
- Building an ethical AI culture requires leadership, incentives, training, and clear escalation paths.

*In the next chapter, we'll explore how to future-proof your sales career as AI continues to evolve, ensuring you remain relevant and valuable in an increasingly automated world.*

# FUTURE-PROOFING YOUR CAREER IN THE AI ERA: A HUMAN'S GUIDE TO STAYING RELEVANT

"My AI will get in touch with your AI and find a solution."

LET'S BE HONEST – AI IS TRANSFORMING CAREERS FASTER than I can transform leftover takeout into a "creative" lunch.

(And trust me, that's impressively fast when you're running late for a Zoom call with your camera accidentally on.)

One day, we're comfortably doing our jobs, and the next, we're watching demos of AI tools that can do parts of our work with terrifying efficiency. It's enough to make you question your career choices while stress-scrolling through job listings... not that I've done that—this week.

Speaking as someone who once accidentally left an AI writing assistant running overnight and woke up to a 10,000-word "creative" story featuring a protagonist who was suspiciously similar to my Bernedoodle, Bernie (complete with his distinctive sock-stealing habit), I understand the anxiety about AI's capabilities.

But here's the delicious truth: AI isn't here to replace professionals—it's here to replace professionals who don't know how to leverage AI.

So grab your favorite beverage (I'm nursing my third coffee because sleep is for people who don't impulse-buy "essential" productivity gadgets at midnight), and let's dig into how you can future-proof your career—whatever it might be—in this brave new world.

**Understanding the AI Transformation: What's Already on the Table**

Before we dive into future-proofing strategies, let's take stock of what AI is already doing across various professions:

- **In Creative Fields** (writing, design, marketing): AI is generating first drafts, creating variations of designs, suggesting headlines, and even producing social media content. It's like having an eager intern who works at the speed of light but occasionally gets things spectacularly wrong.
- **In Knowledge Work** (such as law, finance, and research), AI is reviewing documents, summarizing information, generating reports, and identifying key patterns. It's turning days of work into hours, assuming you don't spend all that saved time just double-checking its work (which we all do).
- **In Technical Roles** (programming, data analysis): AI is generating code, debugging, analyzing massive datasets, and even suggesting optimizations. It's the pair-programming partner who never needs coffee breaks but might occasionally suggest solutions that seem illogical.
- **In Service Industries** (healthcare, education, customer support): AI is handling routine inquiries, creating personalized learning plans, analyzing symptoms, and managing scheduling. It's like having an efficient assistant who sometimes completely misunderstands basic human emotions.

Like that time I tried to cook a soufflé while simultaneously joining a conference call (spoiler alert: both collapsed dramatically), attempting to ignore these AI advancements will only lead to disaster. But embracing them? That's where opportunity lives.

### The Human Ingredients AI (Still) Can't Replace

Here's the good news: there are fundamental human capabilities that AI still struggles with, and these are your ingredients for career longevity:

#### 1. Emotional Intelligence and Relationship Building

AI can analyze sentiment, but it can't truly understand complex human emotions or build authentic relationships. It can't read subtle body language during a tense meeting or sense when a colleague needs encouragement versus space.

Trust me on this one—I once let an AI craft a "supportive" message to a teammate going through a tough time, and it chose precisely the wrong moment to include an inspirational quote about "pushing through obstacles." To the person dealing with an actual physical injury... I'm still apologizing. Some situations demand human sensitivity.

#### 2. Contextual Judgment and Ethical Decision-Making

AI excels at pattern recognition but struggles with context-dependent judgments and ethical reasoning that professionals make daily. It can't weigh complex trade-offs between competing values or understand nuanced cultural considerations.

(Speaking of judgment—Bernie has witnessed more ethical dilemmas than any dog should. He's practically earned a philosophy degree just from listening to me talk through work challenges during our walks.)

### 3. Creative Problem-Solving and Innovation

While AI can generate variations on existing ideas, true innovation—connecting seemingly unrelated concepts to create something novel—remains distinctly a human trait. AI doesn't have those shower moments when you suddenly realize the perfect solution to a problem you've been wrestling with for weeks.

Like that time my smart home system announced, "Time for bed!" right in the middle of a breakthrough brainstorming session at 11 PM. No algorithm could have known I was finally figuring out a complex problem, but somehow I turned that interruption into an insight about setting better boundaries. (The smart speaker, however, has been permanently muted.)

### 4. Adaptability and Learning in Ambiguous Situations

AI models are trained on existing data and struggle with truly novel situations. Your ability to navigate ambiguity, decide with incomplete information, and adapt to changing circumstances is something algorithms find challenging.

**Your Recipe for Future-Proofing Any Career**

So how do you ensure you remain valuable as AI continues to evolve? Here's my fail-proof recipe (unlike my infamous "experimental" curry that even Bernie refused to acknowledge as food):

- **1. Become an AI-Human Collaboration Expert**
    - Don't just use AI tools reluctantly—master them in ways that amplify your unique human capabilities. This means:
        - Understanding what AI tools in your field can and cannot do effectively
        - Developing workflows that leverage AI for efficiency while preserving your human touch
        - Knowing when to rely on AI and when to rely on your judgment
    - Trust me, as a certified tech enthusiast who once spent four hours setting up AI automation that would have taken 20 minutes to do manually (not my finest moment), finding this balance takes practice. But it's worth it.

- **2. Strengthen Your Uniquely Human Skills**
    - As AI handles more routine aspects of work, your distinctly human capabilities become more valuable:
        - Develop deeper emotional intelligence and relationship-building skills
        - Sharpen your ethical reasoning and contextual judgment
        - Cultivate your creativity and innovative thinking
        - Practice critical thinking and decision-making in ambiguous situations
    - (Like the time I remembered a colleague mentioned their child's art show and asked about it weeks later—something no AI would have flagged as necessary—which ultimately led to a collaborative project that transformed our department.) Sometimes it's the little human connections that create the most significant opportunities.
- **3. Become a Continuous Learning Machine**
    - The half-life of professional skills is shrinking faster than my willpower at a farmers' market. To stay relevant:
        - Dedicate time each week to learning about AI developments in your field
        - Join communities where professionals share insights about working alongside AI

        - Experiment with new tools and approaches before you're forced to
    - Speaking as someone who resisted using speech-to-text for years (typing everything manually felt "more accurate," said my delusional past self), I can tell you that proactive learning beats reactive panic every time.
- **4. Position Yourself at the Human-AI Interface**
    - Some of the most valuable future roles will exist at the intersection of human expertise and AI capabilities:
        - Develop skills in "translating" between technical AI capabilities and human needs
        - Learn to effectively prompt, guide, and quality-check AI outputs in your domain
        - Build expertise in identifying which problems are suitable for AI and which require human handling
    - This is the professional equivalent of knowing exactly when to use a food processor versus chopping by hand – technically nuanced, impossible to automate fully, and incredibly valuable when done right.
- **5. Cultivate Your Brand Around Human Value-Add**
    - In an AI-saturated world, your reputation for distinctly human contributions becomes crucial:

        - Share thoughtful insights that demonstrate your judgment and creativity
        - Become known for a specific type of expertise or problem-solving approach
        - Build a network that recognizes and vouches for your human value-add
    - Like that time I became known as the "go-to person" for translating complex technical changes into language client-facing teams could understand (a random niche I fell into after one successful presentation and many late nights with technical documentation and emergency chocolate supplies).

### The Sweet Finish: Embracing Your AI-Enhanced Future

The future of work isn't human OR AI—it's human PLUS AI. The most successful professionals will be those who embrace these tools while also leveraging their uniquely human capabilities.

Think of it like the perfect meal—AI handles the repetitive prep work and data analysis, freeing you up to focus on the creative flourishes, meaningful connections, and complex judgments that make your professional contribution valuable.

Will there be awkward moments as we figure this out? Absolutely. (Ask my smart home system that ordered "low inventory items" automatically and somehow determined I needed 12 bottles of hot sauce. Thanks, but no thanks, HAL.)

But if you follow this recipe for future-proofing your career —embracing AI collaboration, strengthening human skills, continuously learning, positioning yourself at the human-AI interface, and building your brand—you'll find yourself more valuable than ever in tomorrow's workplace.

And if all else fails, you can always join me in my backup career plan: training AI systems to understand when humans are joking versus being serious. (Bernie thinks it's a brilliant idea, but then again, he also thinks dirty socks are gourmet treats, so take that endorsement with a grain of salt.)

Now, if you'll excuse me, I need to check on what my AI calendar assistant may have committed me to while I was writing this.

Trust me on this one – the future of work is delightfully human, intelligently automated, and full of possibilities for those willing to adapt their professional recipe for success.

# FINAL OVERVIEW: THE AI ADVANTAGE – ADAPT, LEVERAGE, AND LEAD

By now, you've seen how AI is revolutionizing the professional world—whether you're in marketing, sales, law, healthcare, education, or running your own business. You've explored the tools that save time, increase productivity, and reduce mental overload. You've also seen that AI isn't a magic bullet—it's a force multiplier. If you know how to use it, it will make you smarter, faster, and more efficient.

But here's the real takeaway:

AI won't replace professionals. But professionals who use AI will replace those who don't.

Those who understand how to leverage AI will outperform, out-innovate, and outlast their competitors. Those who refuse to adapt will struggle to keep up.

So let's break this down one last time:

### What You've Learned in This Book

**AI isn't coming—it's already here.** It's transforming how professionals work, reducing inefficiencies, and giving early adopters a significant advantage.

**AI doesn't replace human intelligence—it enhances it.** You still need strategy, creativity, and decision-making skills. AI is here to handle the repetitive, time-consuming tasks so you can focus on high-value work.

**AI is industry-specific.** The way a marketer uses AI isn't the same as a lawyer or a doctor. That's why we broke down exactly how AI is being used in each profession—so you can tailor AI adoption to your field.

**AI is an assistant, not an autopilot.** It can draft emails, contracts, and reports—but you have to review, edit, and apply human judgment. AI is fast, but it's not always accurate.

**The AI tools covered in this book are just the beginning.** New tools are emerging every month. The best professionals will stay ahead of trends, experiment, and adapt.

### Your AI Implementation Plan – What to Do Next

Reading about AI is excellent, but **actual results come from action.** Here's a step-by-step guide to ensure you're not just learning about AI—you're integrating it into your work.

#### Step 1: Identify Where AI Can Help You Immediately

Start by asking yourself:

- What repetitive, time-consuming tasks take up most of my day?
- What tasks do I struggle with or dislike that AI could improve?
- Where could AI make me more efficient without reducing quality?

**Example:**

If you spend hours writing emails,
use ChatGPT or Lavender AI to draft them faster.

If you manually process contracts, test an AI contract analysis tool.

If customer inquiries take up too much time, deploy an AI chatbot.

| Task / Workflow | Time Spent Weekly | Annoyance Level 😤 (1–10) | Could AI Help? (Y/N) |
|---|---|---|---|
| Example: Writing social posts | 4 hours | 8 | Yes |

### Step 2: Choose the Right AI Tools for Your Industry

There's no one-size-fits-all AI tool. The AI that helps a doctor won't be helpful to a sales executive. Revisit your industry's chapter and start with the 2-3 AI tools that best fit your needs.

- **For Marketers** → AI-powered content tools like **Jasper, Copy.ai, or Canva AI**
- **For Sales Professionals** → AI-driven CRMs like **HubSpot Sales Hub AI** and **HubSpot Smart CRM.**
- **For Lawyers** → AI-powered legal assistants like **Casetext's CoCounsel** for research and drafting, and **Evisort** for contract analysis and management.

- **For Healthcare Providers** → AI transcription and diagnostic tools like **Nuance DAX or Viz.ai**
- **For Educators** → AI lesson planning and grading tools like **MagicSchool AI or Gradescope**
- **For Small Business Owners** → AI-powered automation tools like **ManyChat, QuickBooks AI, and Xero AI**

Start small, test **one or two tools**, and expand as you gain confidence.

| Goal / Need | AI Tool(s) to Try | Start Date | Notes |
|---|---|---|---|
| Draft emails faster | ChatGPT, Lavender.ai | | |
| Find leads or warm up prospects | Apollo AI, Regie.ai, Seamless.AI | | |
| Automate social content | Taplio, Canva Magic Write | | |
| Reduce meeting fatigue | Fireflies.ai, Otter.ai | | |
| Write better blog content | Jasper, Copy.ai, Claude | | |

## Step 3: Automate Small Tasks, Then Scale Up

- AI adoption should feel like adding a superpowered assistant—not an overwhelming shift.
- Start by automating simple tasks, then scale up to bigger AI-driven changes.

## Step 3: Set a Simple 30-Day Experiment

*Choose ONE task and run an "AI test" for 30 days.*

Pick a task: ______________________________

AI tool(s) you'll try: _________________________

How will you measure success? (Time saved? Output?)

________________________________________

When will you review the results?

_________________

> ***Month 1:*** *Use AI for basic automation (drafting emails, summarizing documents).*
> ***Month 2:*** *Implement AI for research and decision-making (SEO tools, sales forecasting).*
> ***Month 3:*** *Expand AI to optimize workflows (automated chatbots, predictive analytics).*

> *The goal? Let AI handle the busywork so you can focus on high-value work.*

### Step 4: Decide How to Reinforce & Scale

*Now that AI's working, how will you expand its impact?*

- Document the workflow
- Train your VA/team/partner

- Upgrade to paid version (if needed)
- Use AI for weekly planning
- Add another tool to your stack

**Step 5: Stay Ahead—Keep Learning & Experimenting**

The best professionals will stay ahead of AI trends and update their toolkit regularly.

> ***Follow AI news*** *– stay updated on new tools and features that could benefit your work.*
> ***Join AI communities*** *– LinkedIn, Reddit, and online forums - to share insights on best AI practices.*
> ***Test new tools quarterly*** *– set aside time every few months to evaluate new AI options.*

The professionals who keep learning, adapting, and experimenting will be the ones leading in their fields.

When I first started exploring the world of AI, it felt like a mix of magic and chaos. For every "wow" moment, there was an equally confusing or frustrating one (and yes, my dog Bernie has witnessed more than his fair share of both). I wrote this book to be the guide I wish I'd had—a straightforward, no-nonsense map to navigating this powerful new territory.

I hope that you close this book feeling not just informed, but equipped. Equipped to experiment, to adapt, and to integrate these tools in a way that feels authentic to you. Remember, the goal isn't to become more like a machine, but to use machines to become more human—more creative, more strategic, and more connected.

The conversation around AI is constantly evolving, and now you're a part of it. Thank you for taking this journey with me. Now, make your mark.

---

# COMPLETE RESOURCE SECTION: AI TOOLS FOR PRODUCTIVITY, BUSINESS, AND CREATIVITY REFERENCED

This section compiles every AI tool mentioned in this book, along with their official website links and brief descriptions. Each link has been verified for accuracy.

## AI Writing Assistants

This table compares general-purpose AI writing tools, focusing on their primary strengths, from creative drafting to marketing copy and grammatical precision.

| Tool | Primary Function | Best For... | Key Differentiator |
|---|---|---|---|
| **ChatGPT (OpenAI)** | General-purpose conversational AI | Quick drafts, brainstorming, summarizing, rewriting | The "Swiss Army knife" versatility; handles a huge range of tasks. |
| **Claude (Anthropic)** | Advanced conversational AI | Nuanced, long-form content (reports, articles) | Superior tone coherence and handling of complex instructions. |
| **Jasper** | Marketing & Sales Copywriting | Creating branded marketing content at scale | Pre-built templates for ads, emails, and blog posts. |
| **Wordtune** | Rephrasing & Tone Adjustment | Improving existing text, overcoming writer's block | Focuses on rewriting and suggesting alternative phrasing, not just generating. |
| **Grammarly** | Grammar & Clarity Assistant | Polishing final drafts for correctness and style | Advanced grammar, plagiarism, and tone detection. |
| **Lex (by Every)** | Collaborative Writing Partner | Writers who want AI suggestions within their workflow | Functions like a "Google Docs with AI," offering suggestions as you type. |

- **ChatGPT (OpenAI)** –
- **Claude (Anthropic)**

- **Lex (by Every)** –
- **Grammarly** –
- **Jasper** –
- **Wordtune** –

## AI Research & Information Processing

These tools are designed to find, synthesize, and manage information, from academic research to daily news.

| Tool | Primary Function | Best For... | Key Differentiator |
|---|---|---|---|
| **Perplexity AI** | Conversational Search Engine | Getting quick, cited answers to complex questions | Provides direct answers with source links, like a research assistant. |
| **Elicit** | Academic Research Assistant | Researchers and students summarizing scientific papers | Tailored specifically for analyzing and finding concepts in academic literature. |
| **Consensus** | Scientific Consensus Finder | Finding evidence-based answers from research papers | Searches for and surfaces findings directly from published studies. |
| **Readwise** | Reading & Digesting Tool | Centralizing highlights from articles, books, and reports | Turns your reading material into a digestible, reviewable knowledge base. |
| **Connected Papers** | Research Discovery Tool | Visually exploring academic landscapes | Creates a graph of related papers to discover seminal and new works. |
| **Mem.ai** | Self-organizing Knowledge Base | Automatically connecting and resurfacing related notes | Uses AI to find links between your notes without manual tagging. |

- Perplexity AI –
- Elicit –

- **Consensus –**
- **Readwise**
- **Connected Papers**
- **Mem.ai**

## AI Meeting Assistants

These tools act as your assistant for meetings, handling everything from note-taking to sentiment analysis.

| Tool | Primary Function | Best For... | Key Differentiator |
| --- | --- | --- | --- |
| **Otter.ai** | Transcription & Summarization | Individuals needing accurate, real-time meeting notes | High-quality transcription with speaker identification. |
| **Fireflies.ai** | Automated Meeting Notes | Teams wanting automated summaries and action items | Joins meetings automatically and sends detailed summaries post-call. |
| **Airgram** | Note-taking & Action Tracking | Collaborative teams needing structured meeting outputs | Focuses on creating structured notes, agendas, and trackable action items. |
| **Sembly AI** | Team Meeting Analytics | Managers wanting deeper insights into team dynamics | Provides sentiment analysis and tracks key topics across meetings. |

- **Otter.ai**
- **Fireflies.ai**
- **Airgram**
- **Sembly AI**

## AI Voice-to-Text & Dictation Tools

This category focuses on the core task of converting spoken words into written text, with options for original use cases from personal notes to developer APIs.

| Tool | Primary Function | Best For... | Key Differentiator |
|---|---|---|---|
| **Whisper (OpenAI)** | Speech Recognition System | Developers needing a highly accurate transcription model | Open-source and known for its exceptional accuracy across many languages. |
| **Otter Voice Notes** | Personal Dictation | Individuals wanting to capture and transcribe thoughts on the go | Combines dictation with the summarization power of Otter.ai. |
| **Rev.ai** | Developer-focused Transcription | Businesses needing industrial-strength transcription API | Offers high accuracy with features like global language support and timestamps. |
| **Just Press Record** | Simple iOS Dictation | Apple users needing a simple, one-tap recording app | Simplicity and seamless iCloud synchronization. |

- **Whisper (OpenAI)**
- **Otter Voice Notes** –
- **Rev.ai**
- **Just Press Record.**

## AI Task Management Systems

These tools don't just list your tasks; they help you prioritize, schedule, and organize them intelligently.

| Tool | Primary Function | Best For... | Key Differentiator |
|---|---|---|---|
| **Todoist** | Smart Task Management | Individuals needing intelligent task capture and organization | Natural language processing for easy task creation (e.g., "Finish report by Friday"). |
| **Motion** | AI-powered Scheduler | Professionals who live by their calendar | Uses AI to automatically build your daily schedule and reprioritize tasks. |
| **Reclaim.ai** | Intelligent Time Blocking | Teams and individuals trying to protect focus time | Automatically finds the best time for tasks, habits, and meetings. |
| **Akiflow** | Unified Task & Calendar Hub | Users wanting to consolidate tasks from multiple apps | Pulls tasks from various tools (like Slack, Gmail) into one central command center. |

- **Todoist**
- **Motion.**
- **Reclaim.ai**
- **Akiflow**

## AI Decision Support Tools

These tools enhance strategic thinking, reduce bias, and help teams and individuals make better, more data-driven decisions.

| Tool | Primary Function | Best For... | Key Differentiator |
|---|---|---|---|
| **Coda AI** | Strategic Planning Assistant | Teams building documents, plans, and roadmaps | Integrates AI directly into collaborative documents for planning and modeling. |
| **Unanimous AI** | Group Decision-making | Teams needing to reach an optimized consensus | Uses "Swarm Intelligence" to amplify a group's collective wisdom. |
| **Foresight Strategy** | Strategic Business Planning | Leaders and strategists doing long-term planning | AI-powered platform specifically for building and testing business strategies. |
| **Clearer Thinking** | Cognitive Bias Reduction | Individuals wanting to improve their reasoning skills | Provides tools and exercises to identify and overcome common mental biases. |

- **Coda AI**
- **Unanimous AI**
- **Foresight Strategy**
- **Clearer Thinking Tools.**

## AI Productivity & Focus Tools

This category focuses on tools that help you manage your attention, minimize distractions, and get into a state of deep work.

| Tool | Primary Function | Best For... | Key Differentiator |
|---|---|---|---|
| **Supernormal** | Automated Note-taking | Individuals who need to quickly document conversations | AI listens and automatically writes detailed notes for you. |
| **Magic AI Assistant** | Virtual Task Delegation | Busy professionals needing an on-demand assistant | Text-based assistant that can handle tasks like booking, research, and scheduling. |
| **Zapier AI** | Workflow Automation | Connecting different apps and services together | Allows you to build AI-powered "Zaps" to automate cross-app workflows. |
| **Process Street** | Process & Checklist Automation | Teams needing to standardize recurring workflows | Uses AI to help create and manage checklists and standard operating procedures. |

- **Focus App**
- **Centered**
- **FlowTime AI**
- **Sunsama**
- **Notion AI**

## AI Delegation & Automation Tools

These tools help you automate workflows and delegate tasks, acting as a force multiplier for your efforts.

| Tool | Primary Function | Best For... | Key Differentiator |
| --- | --- | --- | --- |
| **Supernormal** | Automated Note-taking | Individuals who need to quickly document conversations | AI listens and automatically writes detailed notes for you. |
| **Magic AI Assistant** | Virtual Task Delegation | Busy professionals needing an on-demand assistant | Text-based assistant that can handle tasks like booking, research, and scheduling. |
| **Zapier AI** | Workflow Automation | Connecting different apps and services together | Allows you to build AI-powered "Zaps" to automate cross-app workflows. |
| **Process Street** | Process & Checklist Automation | Teams needing to standardize recurring workflows | Uses AI to help create and manage checklists and standard operating procedures. |

- **Supernormal**
- **Magic AI Assistant**
- **Zapier AI Integration**
- **Process Street**

## AI Email Management & Optimization

This category includes tools designed to help you conquer your inbox, from faster replies to automated prioritization.

| Tool | Primary Function | Best For... | Key Differentiator |
|---|---|---|---|
| **Superhuman** | High-speed Email Client | Professionals who see email as a core productivity tool | Designed for speed with AI-powered features like triage and summarization. |
| **SaneBox** | Email Filtering & Prioritization | Users with overflowing inboxes needing automated cleanup | AI learns your habits and automatically filters unimportant emails. |
| **Front** | Team Communication Hub | Companies needing to manage shared inboxes (e.g., support@) | AI helps route messages and provides context for team collaboration. |
| **Shortwave** | Smart Email Management | Users who want a smarter, more organized inbox experience | AI bundles related emails and helps you draft replies instantly. |

- **Superhuman**
- **SaneBox.**
- **Front**
- **Shortwave**

## AI Calendar Optimization

These tools go beyond simple scheduling to intelligently manage your most valuable asset: your time.

| Tool | Primary Function | Best For... | Key Differentiator |
|---|---|---|---|
| **Reclaim.ai** | Intelligent Time Blocking | Balancing meetings, tasks, and personal habits | The best tool for automatically finding flexible time for deep work. |
| **Motion** | Dynamic Task Scheduling | Task-driven professionals who need an automated daily plan | Creates a full schedule and dynamically re-arranges it when conflicts arise. |
| **Clockwise** | Smart Meeting Scheduler | Teams looking to optimize schedules and create focus time | Automatically resolves meeting conflicts and shifts meetings to open up blocks of time. |
| **Trevor AI** | Time Management & Planning | Individuals who want a simple, AI-powered planning app | Uses AI to help you schedule your to-do list into a realistic time-blocked plan. |

- **Reclaim.ai.**
- **Motion.**
- **Clockwise**
- **Trevor AI**

## AI Follow-Up & Networking Tools

These tools help you manage your professional relationships and ensure no critical connections or opportunities fall through the cracks.

| Tool | Primary Function | Best For... | Key Differentiator |
|---|---|---|---|
| **FollowUp.cc** | Email Follow-up Automation | Individuals needing simple, reliable follow-up reminders | Simple commands to schedule follow-ups directly from your inbox. |
| **Streak for Gmail** | CRM inside Gmail | Salespeople and teams who operate primarily out of Gmail | Turns your inbox into a CRM with tracking and follow-up sequences. |
| **Boomerang** | Email Scheduling & Reminders | General users wanting more control over their email | AI helps you write better emails and find the optimal time to send them. |
| **Clay** | Relationship Management | Serious networkers who want to build strong connections | Acts as a "personal chief of staff" by pulling in data from all your networks. |

- **FollowUp.cc**
- **Streak for Gmail**
- **Boomerang**
- **Clay**

## AI for Sales & Marketing

This table compares tools specifically built for the top of the sales and marketing funnel, from lead generation to conversation analysis.

| Tool | Primary Function | Best For... | Key Differentiator |
|---|---|---|---|
| **Seamless.AI** | Lead Generation Platform | Sales teams needing a high volume of accurate contact data | Real-time search engine for finding verified cell phones and emails. |
| **Lavender.ai** | Sales Email Coach | Sales reps wanting to improve their outreach effectiveness | Provides real-time feedback to help you write emails that get replies. |
| **Gong.ai** | Conversation Intelligence | Sales managers and teams wanting to analyze call performance | Records and analyzes sales calls to identify what top performers are doing differently. |
| **Jasper** | Marketing Content Creation | Marketing teams needing to create high-quality, on-brand content | Optimized for creating marketing materials like ad copy, blog posts, and social media updates. |

- **Seamless.AI**
- **Lavender.ai**
- **Gong.ai**
- **Jasper**

This list compiles all AI tools mentioned throughout the book, along with descriptions, to assist professionals in optimizing productivity, creativity, and efficiency. As tools change more frequently than my Bernie hides my socks, I will maintain a "live" updated site you can reference. Please check the official websites for those updates and other resources!

# EXCLUSIVE TOOLS FOR YOUR USE CREATED FOR OUR READERS

When you realize
learning AI jargon
could take all weekend.

## AI Sales Tools Comparison Spreadsheet:

This spreadsheet provides a comprehensive comparison of various AI sales tools, including categories, pricing, ratings (1-5 scale), best use cases, and typical implementation times. Utilize the built-in filters to sort by category, price range, or team size and find the ideal AI sales tool for your specific needs.

SCAN ME!

*AI Sales Tools Comparison Spreadsheet:*

## SalesAI Readiness Pro - AI Sales Assessment Tool

Is your sales process leaking revenue? Before investing in any AI tool, it's essential to understand where the real opportunities lie. The SalesAI Readiness Pro is your diagnostic toolkit. This powerful assessment identifies the specific areas in your sales funnel that are ripe for AI-powered optimization. Stop wasting money on the wrong solutions and get the clarity you need to choose the right tools that will give you an immediate competitive edge.

*Sales AI Readiness Pro - AI Sales Assessment Tool*

## AI Tool Selection Decision Tree

Overwhelmed by the sheer number of AI tools on the market? You're not alone. The AI Tool Selection Decision Tree is your personal consultant, designed to cut through the noise. This interactive guide walks you through a series of simple, strategic questions about your goals, budget, and workflow. Instead of endless research, get a curated shortlist of the best-fit AI tools for your specific needs in minutes. It's the most innovative way to make your next AI investment.

SCAN ME!

*AI Tool Selection Decision Tree*

## 100 AI Prompts That Will Revolutionize Your Business

Ready to go beyond basic AI questions? This is your playbook. "100 AI Prompts That Will Revolutionize Your Business" is more than a list—it's a masterclass in crafting effective AI prompts. Discover how to command your AI to generate viral marketing campaigns, draft persuasive legal arguments, build strategic business frameworks, and much more. Stop getting generic answers and start getting game-changing insights that will put you miles ahead of the competition.

SCAN ME!

*00 AI Prompts That Will Revolutionize Your Business*

The Ultimate AI Business Growth Prompt Collection

Curated for Maximum Impact and Effectiveness

I had over 800 prompts collected for business growth-related purposes. To make that collection useful, I instructed my AI assistant to do a thorough analysis and narrow it down to the best and most necessary prompts. Here is that select list by category. Click the link above

Table of Contents

SCAN ME!

*The Ultimate AI Business Growth Prompt Collection*

Made in United States
North Haven, CT
04 November 2026

21766917R00153